JESUS
The Mantra of God

Already published:

Abhinavagupta, the Kula Ritual
as elaborated in Chapter 29 of the Tantraloka
Delhi, Motilal Banarsidass, 2003
ISBN 81-208-1979-9   xv+532 pp.

JESUS
The Mantra of God

*An exploration of
mantra meditation*

JOHN DUPUCHE

**Foreword by
Laurence Freeman** OSB

David Lovell Publishing
Melbourne Australia

First published in 2005 by

David Lovell Publishing

PO Box 822 Ringwood

Victoria 3134 Australia

Tel +61 3 9879 1433

Fax +61 3 9879 1348

Cover painting: Pat Negri sss, 'Yahweh Painting', oil, acrylic
and gold leaf on canvas board, 1992-98, 44 x 22 cm.

Design by David Lovell Publishing

Typeset in 12/17 Perpetua

Printed and bound in Australia by Openbook Print

National Library of Australia
Cataloguing-in-Publication data

Dupuche, John R.
   Jesus, the mantra of God : an exploration of mantra meditation.
   ISBN 1 86355 1107
   1. Meditation, 2. Prayers, 1, Title
242

With thanks and appreciation
this work is dedicated to
my extended family:

Françoise and her husband Peter (dec.),
René and his wife Wendy,
Bertrand (dec.) and his wife Angela,
and Anne-Marie (1945-1947),
their children and grand-children.

CONTENTS

PART II

Contents

PREFACE

In a world of increasingly dangerous polarisation it has become more and more urgent to discover humanity's deepest levels of communion. So many of our crises — ecological, economic, ethnic, religious and social — are being compounded by deliberate ignorance and denial. Fundamentalism, rising in many religions, is a profoundly disturbing and saddening phenomenon. A contemplative consciousness is needed to confront the forces of denial and to open the hearts of those who exclude.

Anything therefore that points us towards the experience of our grounding human unity as a family of God — with all its diverse ways of expressing this fact — is to be welcomed and encouraged. Meditation is perhaps the simplest and most universal key to this experience of our common ground. While enlightening us to this core human communion, it at the same time respects and affirms the uniqueness of each religious tradition in which it is found.

Meditation is a universal spiritual practice — a wisdom tasted in the practice. In some form it is found at the foundation level of all religions, including aboriginal traditions. Jesus himself was clearly a teacher of contemplation, urging his followers to be aware of the dangers of external religiosity that had lost connection with the heart. In the Sermon on the Mount, he points us towards interiority, silence, trust, attention and living in the present moment — the essential elements of contemplation — as the true meaning of prayer. Without appreciating this central thrust of his teaching, his other doctrine of non-violence is relegated to the backburner of religion as an idealistically impossible practice.

John Dupuche has made an important contribution to the awareness of the universality of meditation. He also sees its importance for truly changing the mind of our time. Learned in the oriental traditions, he has been able through his Christian faith to suggest many connections from these great springs of the human spirit with Christian faith and practice.

He refers to the pioneering work in this field begun by John Main thirty years ago and the way this has now grown into a worldwide ecumenical community. He is right in pointing out that Fr John first encountered the practice of meditation as a spiritual discipline through an encounter with a personal teacher in the East. While remaining a Christian (and wanting to meditate in order to deepen his faith and understanding of Christ) he engaged at first with meditation in its universal form. But this helped him later to recognise the Christian manifestation of meditation (*oratio pura*) in the mystical tradition of the early church and monastic fathers. This then plunged him deep into the stream of scriptural and theological meanings released by the experience of silence, stillness and simplicity practised in poverty of spirit and faith in Jesus.

John Main always retained a deep love and reverence for the religions of the East. But his teaching of Christian Meditation was based integrally on the mystical and contemplative wisdom of Christianity itself. Nothing was more important for him than for the Church — ecumenically speaking — to reawaken to its own immense spiritual depths. Dogmatic theology and sacramental life do not, however, in this vision, become less important. In fact they become recharged with meaning and power to the same degree that the contemplative experience deepens and opens the mind and heart in faith and love.

John Main's approach to teaching the Christian tradition of the mantra differs from John Dupuche in a number of interesting and suggestive ways that show how deep and wide the spiritual field is. While Fr John did not recommend the 'positioning of the mantra', John Dupuche describes the Hindu practice of doing so. John Main did not encourage the meditator to pay attention to the chakras, except the simple advice to 'say the mantra in your heart'. He taught the meditator to say the mantra without self-consciously observing or analyzing the practice, the better to see the fruits of the practice in their life. Among these fruits none is more important than the active growth of compassion — as of course John Dupuche also points out. John Main recommended a perhaps more simple and more single-pointed attention to the mantra in the apophatic tradition of the Christian Desert. He liked to quote St Antony of the Desert who said that 'the monk who knows that he is praying is not truly praying but the monk who does not know that he is praying is truly praying'.

So, I sense that John Dupuche is addressing this question of 'experience' a little differently from John Main. But in his own way he too will connect with the search of many seekers today for experience in spiritual practice. In the way John Dupuche does so he can help to reconnect many Christians who have been in exile from the church and have learned much from the East to return to the Christian *sangha* — if and when they feel so called, and as many and in increasing numbers do.

He also employs a careful but not pedantic style and language of spiritual practice which moves naturally and lucidly into a more allegorical style in the second half of the book. I hear echoes here of the early Alexandrian style of theology. Rooted in the practice of prayer it opens the mind to deeper levels of scriptural meaning. Meanings are followed through from the historical and cerebral levels to more mystical depths where all levels of consciousness are unified in the spirit. I particularly enjoyed the beautiful and fresh commentaries on the liturgical seasons in their mutually enriching relationship with the practice of meditation.

The progress of the book, from practice to faith, is itself a powerful reminder that prayer can never be reduced to a technique. It is always an ever deeper entry into the mystery of the life of Christ in the spirit while remaining rooted always in the historical reality of the Incarnation. By showing the prayer of one word — the 'monologistos prayer' of the ancient church — can initiate and guide this journey into union with Christ, John Dupuche will find many grateful readers.

Laurence Freeman OSB

The World Community for Christian Meditation

www.wccm.org

Introduction

The story of John Main (1926-1982) is well known. Whilst in the Far East with the British Colonial Service in Malaya, he learned to meditate with a Hindu monk who taught him the practice of reciting (*japa*) the mantra as a means of entering into the depths of the Divine Mystery.

On his return to England he became a Benedictine monk and later began to teach the mantra from his Christian monastic tradition of contemplative prayer. Then in 1977 he accepted an invitation from the Archdiocese of Montreal to start a Benedictine community there for the practice and teaching of Christian meditation. He rooted this in the teaching of John Cassian and the Desert Fathers who recommended the constant repetition of a 'formula' such as 'O God come to my assistance' (Psalm 69:2).

He taught with great success and wrote with equal flair. However, his death at the full height of his powers cut short the outstanding contribution he was making to the revival of Christian meditation.

This work, *Jesus, the Mantra of God*, does not attempt to describe the many meanings of *mantra*, nor is it an attempt to compare Indian and Christian forms of meditation, nor does it consider the complex question of the relation between Christian revelation and the divine truths communicated in the history of the Indian religions. It simply explores

1

the practice of the mantra promoted by John Main and his disciple Dom Laurence Freeman osb who has continued his teacher's work. The Indian idea of the mantra, about which this author has some knowledge, is like a key to unlock the storeroom from which the disciple of the kingdom brings forth things both new and old (Mtatthew 13:52). The texts which follow stand squarely within the Christian tradition and are simply an elucidation of it.

The essence of John Main's teaching, and that of the World Community for Christian Meditation which continues his work under the guidance of Laurence Freeman, is commonly expressed as follows:

> Sit down, sit still and upright. Close your eyes lightly. Sit relaxed but alert. Breathe calmly and regularly. Silently, interiorly begin to say a single word. We recommend the prayer-phrase 'MA–RA–NA–THA'. Recite it as syllables of equal length. Listen to it as you say, gently but continuously. Do not think or imagine anything — spiritual or otherwise. If thoughts and images come, these are distractions at the time of meditation, so keep returning to simply saying the word. Meditate each morning and evening for between 20 and 30 minutes.

Thus in Part I, after some introductory considerations on faith, which is the basis of all prayer, the mantra is explored in its various aspects, for it is not a 'coat-hanger' on which one hangs things which have no essential relationship to it, rather it bears all the qualities of the human word, indeed of the divine Word. Likewise, 'breath' is a rich term and not just a bodily function. Again, the body is not some object to be 'parked' on a chair. Mantra, breath and body influence each other and together form a unity which leads to the One God.

Nor is mantra-meditation a plinth on which the vast structure of Christian spirituality is placed without any organic connection. Rather, mantra-meditation, properly understood, in itself leads into all the Mysteries, just as the fertile ground yields a rich harvest (Matthew 13:23).

This short book is a help to understanding and appreciating the profound significance of a simple act.

Part II shows the intricate relationship between the cycle of the liturgical year and the daily practice of mantra-meditation. The events of the liturgical year teach the meditators the essential meaning of their recitation, while the practice of meditation allows a person to participate more consciously in the various aspects of the Mass. Mass and meditation are not opposites, nor even alternatives but lead to each other. The outer and the inner are essentially related: the inner becomes real when it is expressed; the outer remains superficial if it does not spring from the heart. Indeed, public prayer and private prayer are both required if the universal call to holiness is to be heard. Part II, therefore, explores mantra-meditation in various ways, sometimes by reliving the sacred story, sometimes by showing the spiritual impact of a liturgical period.

The practice of mantra meditation also provides scope for the development of a theological language based on the mantra and particularly on the very act of recitation.

One can assume that John Main was aware of the other aspects of the Indian teaching on the mantra even though these do not find expression in his own presentation of the tradition. One could mention, for example the placing (*ny¡sa*) of the mantra on the various centres (*cakra*) of the body, to bless them and empower them, to purify and redeem them. It is an example of the power of the Word.

Finally, whilst the book is concerned with mantra-meditation, the Appendix entitled 'visualisation' makes allowance for those whose approach is visual as well as verbal. Sight as well as sound can lead into the depths.

I would like to thank Ted Waterman, Patricia Chaves, Breda Hertaeg, Kieran Little and others of the meditation circle at Stella Maris,

Beaumaris, for their companionship in the journey of meditation. These pages are the revision of the texts provided by the author to our meditation meetings during the years 2001–2003. Thanks also go to Ruth Fowler of the World Community for Christian Meditation for reviewing these pages and making valuable suggestions. Thanks also to Swami Sannyasananda for reviewing the section on the chakras and confirming the exactness of their description.

Faith

1. Starting the journey

... faith is the knowledge of things unseen. (Hebrews 11:1)

Meditation is first and foremost an act of faith. Indeed, the very act of taking up the meditative posture is the first step on a long journey into the unknown. What will happen? Will anything happen? What phantasms will arise from the depths of the subconscious? What unresolved issues will arise and shout? What sense of beauty and undiscovered light will appear? It is a journey of confidence despite the uncertainties, for it is based on knowledge. Indeed the journey could not begin unless the goal was in some way already known. The journey starts with concealed knowledge and arrives at full revelation, for 'faith is the knowledge of things unseen'.

Meditation is done with flair, for we can sense the quarry. An interior compass guides us. A music, a soft, compelling music, has begun to call the practitioner away from the noise of ordinary life. So the meditator enters into silence in order to hear more clearly. The busyness of life is abandoned in favour of stillness, so as to sense the interior movement of the Spirit summoning the spirit. Thoughts are abandoned since a higher knowledge is being revealed within.

What inspired the meditator to begin the journey? When did the silent music first stir? What word or image, what example or encouragement won the meditator's confidence and brought out the words, 'Yes, I will go'? Or is the meditator an inconstant traveler saying, 'I will try it and see how it goes', ready to abandon the attempt when difficulties come? What passion is at work? The victory belongs to the brave.

Who will show the way? Books can teach but the presence of the enlightened master gives 'seven-league boots', for the lived example is worth many written pages. Indeed, the presence of a community will help and safeguard, and the contribution of a well-tried tradition will protect against the many traps along the way. But, finally, the going is solitary, alone with the Alone, led by an interior angel, the Spirit at work in the depths of the spirit. Ultimately all books and all human teachers are set aside, so that the Whisper of God is the only guide.

2. Light and dark

Yahweh went before them, by day in the form of a pillar of cloud ... by night in the form of a pillar of fire.
(Exodus 13:21)

Meditation is a journey of faith, which goes by winding paths, alternating light and shade. The initial enthusiasm of meditation dries up and gives way to desolation and the moment of crisis. Many give up, but some continue, for a music is playing in them that they cannot resist, calling them into silence. They go ever deeper and find a level of joy which has not yet been explored. So light and dark continue to alternate till the deepest recesses are explored, the very foundations of the spirit where the Spirit dwells.

Each person's journey is different and there are few signposts. Human guides, though valuable, eventually prove inadequate so that the journey must be made alone with only a spiritual sensitivity to show the way, warning against false starts and dead ends. The journey is done in darkness, with hands outstretched feeling along the darkened corridors so that the spiritual sense eventually becomes highly developed. It alone is of interest: the dark beacon of faith.

Thus a person goes beyond senses and intelligence and even beyond clear revelation into silence. The light of felt joy loses its radiance; the understanding that had become the guide in turn loses its brightness. All else fails and only a luminous darkness leads through the unknown.

This journey is for the strong. It will at last become evident that the Spirit is praying within, choosing the meditator as the temple in which the sacrifice is performed. When joy comes out of nothing, nothing can take it away.

3. Light inaccessible

'Holy, Holy, Holy.' (Isaiah 6:3)

In the journey of faith all received knowledge falls away leaving only the direct experience of the transcendent. All knowledge gained through senses or intellect or tradition loses its impact. Enigma and paradox best describe faith, for it is the knowledge of the unknowable, the immediate perception of the transcendent, an enlightened darkness. Nothing can take it away since it did not come from anything that this world holds. It is not subject to proof or disproof but is directly experienced as a gift. Because faith is so seemingly impossible, so immediate and so deep, it is profoundly satisfying and utterly enjoyable.

When this joy is perceived as a gift given totally beyond our control, the Giver is known as utterly transcendent. In this way, the faith that has led to the depths also communicates a sense of the Transcendent that is beyond reach yet intimated, both known and unknown, and who is acknowledged as 'Holy, Holy, Holy', dwelling in light inaccessible.

A deep silence descends and an immense joy arises.

This gift was given from the beginning, little did the meditator realize. It was indeed the silent sound that resonated at the start and called to the journey of faith. It gave the strength and conviction to leave the familiar and plunge into the unknown.

This gift of faith shows that all is gift.

4. The power of faith

'Were your faith the size of a mustard seed you could say to this mulberry tree, "Be uprooted and planted in the sea", and it would obey you.' (Luke 17.:)

Faith empowers. If faith as small as a mustard seed can move mountains, the faith that has identified with the boundless God makes and remakes both heaven and earth.

Paradoxically, by giving up all ambition and entering into the darkness, the meditator acquires authority over heaven and earth such as was given to him who died and rose again. Dispassion leads to universal concern.

The water and the blood flow from the side of Christ pierced by the lance; power springs from him in death so that the world is renewed. This is experienced in meditation when a certain completeness of faith is reached. It seems that, spontaneously, grace and blessing flow, bringing peace and redemption.

The meditator is not uninvolved. Authority is given such that the meditator can apply the healing rays wherever the heart directs. It is an act of profound intentionality but at one with the inspiring Spirit and the commanding Author of all. This freedom has to be experienced if it is to be properly understood and become available to the meditator.

The power of faith heals what is hurt and continues to be active even when all is healed, for faith lasts. It is also a power enhancing each person, making them more able in turn to enhance the capacity of others so that there is grace upon grace, movement from glory to glory, ever expanding, exponentially.

In fact the power that springs from identity is already present in the eternal Trinity, who commune with each other and acknowledge each other. The journey of faith leads to identity with the Triune God.

The Mantra

Why use a mantra? Mantra-meditation is not necessary for all, but it is necessary for some. Each person must find his or her own path of salvation. For many the spiritual path is followed by 'coming to the help of orphans and widows when they need it' (James 1:27). For those, however, who are called to sit in stillness and allow the Word to penetrate, transforming them into the Word, the mantra is the necessary way. Words are essential to all human beings, since human beings are by nature verbal creatures; but for some recitation is the vehicle of predilection for entering into the depth.

1. Preparing for the mantra

Before the world was made, he chose us ... (Ephesians 1:4)

It is God who meditates. Out of Silence the Word is uttered and the Word is said into Silence. From all eternity God speaks his Word, once and forever. Out of eternity he intends that others should say the same Word, forever.

Silence and Word imply each other. The Word proceeds from the One who is called Father and who can be called Silence since the Word proceeds from him. The Word leads to Silence, where there is complete repose. Thus Silence leads to Word and Word leads to Silence.

Furthermore, it is only by the inspiration of the silent Spirit that the meditator can leave the chatter of the world and recite the mantra without disturbance and so enter into that silence where the Word becomes apparent.

Thus, the practitioner meditates by becoming one with the One who meditates. In the first instance, meditation is not the meditator's doing: 'I am going to lure her and lead her out into the wilderness and speak to her heart' (Hosea 2:16).

Out of his freedom, he freely makes the meditator freely want to meditate. There can be no compulsion, no pressure, no meditating because it is fashionable to do so. Meditation occurs only if it happens freely.

The practitioner is inspired to leave 'Egypt' and its 'melons, leeks, onions and garlic' (Numbers 11:5) and go into the silence of the desert or rather into the solitude of a private space, there to discover the Word that has been said within. That is not just the word of some saint, not even a word from the Bible but the Word that precedes all words, the Word given to the practitioner uniquely, which no one else knows except the Speaker who speaks within.

There is an immense presumption in meditating, an immense faith, indeed a knowledge that the Word is present. Meditation is an enlightenment which has no proof beyond its own self-evidence and whose validity is proven by its effects — 'all her children' (Luke 7:35). To discover the divine Mantra is the practitioner's delight and salvation.

So the meditator leaves the chatter of this world, all the non-mantras bringing dissipation and distraction. The meditator turns away for a while from the over-stimulation of modern times, the pressures and anxieties of family and career. The meditator avoids the disturbance arising from the body when it lacks the harmony of proper diet and exercise and a right attitude to the body.

Meditation is but one form of spiritual practice. All those who follow the spiritual practice that is appropriate to their charism and character will find that their every word becomes a mantra. Mantra-meditation abhors any sense of boasting, for any sense of superiority is an illusion and prevents meditation, which is ultimately a surrender to the One who meditates in us.

Such is the preparation for the Word, the preparation for the Good News, the preparation for the mantra.

2. Receiving the mantra

I taught you what I had been taught myself.
(1 Corinthians 15:3)

A mantra can be a sentence, such as the famous 'Jesus prayer'— 'Lord Jesus, Son of the living God, have mercy on me'. The mantra can be a single word such as *maran atha*, 'The Lord is coming', or *marana tha*, 'Come' — a word that is found in the Bible (I Corinthians 16:22, Revelation 22:17); or even an inarticulate sound, as in the groan of the Spirit (Romans 8:23, 26). It may be said 'aloud or in silence' (Hebrews 5:7). In every case it is an expression.

In the first instance the mantra expresses a tradition, just as language embodies a culture, and to accept a mantra is to assent to the tradition that it encapsulates. Furthermore, to recite the mantra is to come in contact with the one who embodies that tradition. Since the sacred words of the Christian tradition are traced back in some sense to their founder, a mantra from that tradition communicates the person of Jesus Christ, so that the communication of the Christian mantra is a preaching of the Gospel. If Jesus is called 'the Word' he can also be called 'the Mantra'. He is the Mantra of God, of which all other mantras are the limited expression. Thus the ordinary mantra, when properly understood, takes us all the way to the divine Meditator, God himself, the primary reciter of the Mantra.

A mantra can be taken from the printed page of a book or of the Bible; it is best received as a gift from the teacher (guru, which means 'heavy' or 'he who carries weight',) just as the consecrated host is formally given and not left on the altar for the communicants to serve themselves.

In the course of the Rite of Christian Initiation of Adults, which is the paradigm for the baptism of infants, the sacred writings are formally given to the initiand and become the store of sacred words from which the mantra may be chosen as the Spirit indicates. For indeed the word which touches and awakens the sleeping heart is the word the Spirit has chosen for the meditator. It may take the meditator some time to distinguish which word of the Sacred Writ is the chosen word.

However, the time has come for the Christian tradition to emphasize anew the custom of the Desert Fathers according to which the disciple sought instruction personally from the 'Ancient' who was rightly called Abba (father) or Amma (mother) because of the close relationship between them. The practice of mantra-meditation will achieve its fullness only with the rediscovery of the teacher-disciple relationship that existed in the early church and was best exemplified by the group of the Twelve and their master and particularly by the relationship of the Beloved Disciple to Jesus.

The teacher in whom the disciple has placed his faith — and in the practice of the desert fathers and mothers it was the disciple who first chose the teacher, whether that teacher was lay or ordained, female or male — the teacher discerns the spiritual character of the disciple and imparts the word that most fully shows the disciple's hidden self and which will become wings allowing the heart to soar into heaven itself.

The mantra is not just a tool, something that can be taken up but does not essentially belong to oneself. Rather, the mantra is the *expression* of oneself, the phonic expression of one's spirit. Like a mirror it reveals the practitioner. Furthermore, it reveals the whole mystery of God to the practitioner of the mantra — and in this sense is a sacrament.

Does the transmission take place in the course of a ceremony or just spontaneously at some given moment? There are many possibilities. In every case the act of transmission will be a memorable moment: the word is handed over like a life-giving spark, a moment of intimate communion between disciple and teacher.

The more the teacher is united with her mantra, the more powerfully does she communicate it. The mantra is received by the disciple with faith in the teacher who gives it. Otherwise the mantra is powerless. It is received in faith and recited in faith. It is the expression both of the guru's tradition and of the disciple's obedience so that the mantra is the meeting point of teacher and disciple. Thus the mantra, properly speaking, is received in faith by the disciple from the revered teacher at the moment of initiation.

Since the words spoken by Jesus and faithfully relayed by the generations of the church, are 'spirit and life' (John 6:63), the mantra becomes a powerful tool for salvation.

By reciting it in faith, the disciple acquires the power of the teacher and journeys back along the tradition to its source, Jesus, and indeed to the One who sends Jesus, for it is really God who gives the Word as well as the capacity to hear the Word, so that in final analysis it is God who gives the mantra and God who receives it.

3. Beginning the mantra

In the beginning was the Word ... through him all things came to be ... and the Word was made flesh. (John 1:1-14)

Out of the Silence, the Word proceeds. The reciter needs first to enter into that Silence, leaving behind every thought, every ambition and desire, withdrawing the senses and going into the 'desert', like the chosen people leaving the land of Egypt for Sinai, the mountain of covenant.

In the calm of encompassing silence, the disciple becomes aware of that infinite Silence, of the One who 'dwells in light inaccessible' (Eucharistic Prayer IV). The reciter is still, poised in the great emptiness, darkness and space that are at first unnerving. This is the moment of purification, a turning away from all limitations, all fragmentation, all doubts and resentments, and a coming to the beginning of things — the clear air of the desert. To dwell in silence is to dwell in the sweetness of the One who is called the 'Void'. To dwell in God is to be free of all that is not of God. It is a rebirth.

'In the beginning was the Word.' From his silence, the Speaker eternally, once and forever, recites his one Word. The recitation is a resonance within the silence, for silence naturally gives rise to sound. The Word does not lose its essential connection with Silence and so, paradoxically, the Word manifests Silence, so natural and gentle is the utterance.

The start of the mantra is a particularly pregnant moment, full of significance. The recitation of the mantra is an imitation, indeed an experience of the Word arising out of Silence. The very act of saying the mantra is an imitation of the original act of God who utters the Word. By imitating the act, the practitioner becomes like God and comes to union with him. Like the wave, which arises from the ocean and seems to hang suspended and then crashes, the mantra arises out of the silence, it seems to hover and then it is said. The moment of hovering is highly dynamic, intense but not tense. The mantra is recited without effort, naturally, by the gentlest impulse.

In the Word, all is contained. Every possibility is both present in the

Word and transcended by the Word. God did indeed say, 'Let there be light' (Genesis 1:3) and, 'Let there be a vault in the waters' (Genesis 1:6), but there is no limit to what he could have said and there is no necessity for him to have said anything. All springs from his prophetic, projecting Word. 'Through the Word all things came to be.' To say the mantra is to be at the source of everything and of every blessing.

'And the Word was made flesh' (John 1:14). The power of God is shown best in weakness. Therefore it is fitting that the infinite Word become completely vulnerable and take on the particularity of human flesh. The mantra, in being recited, takes on a particular form. The recitation of the mantra leads to a heightened sensitivity to the compassionate mind of God and to an increasing rejection of the disturbances that fill the world. It makes the reciter wish to become part of the world so as to bring the peace of the mantra. It does not mean detachment from the world but involvement in its weakness. By our mantra we too become flesh.

4. Becoming the mantra

The Word was made flesh, he lived among us,
and we saw his glory,
the glory that is his as the only Son of the Father,
full of grace and truth. (John 1:14)

The foundation of mantra-recitation is grace. A mantra is wholeheartedly received only under the impulse of grace, and is effectively recited only under the same impulse, for it is God who recites in the reciter.

However, the mantra, ideally given by the teacher personally and individually to the disciple, as mentioned earlier, is imparted not to an empty shell but to a person with a history, a character and a particular measure of grace. The mantra, therefore, takes on the characteristics of the one who receives it. Similarly, and for the same reason, the mantra has the quality of the teacher who gives it. Thus the mantra expresses both the teacher and the disciple who both must be of one mind and heart if a mantra is truly to be communicated.

You only truly receive what you really are. What resonance does the mantra have for you? What does it really express, what attitude, what hope, what insight, what emotion, what quality of energy? Your mantra is the 'white stone' (Revelation 2:17) on which your name is written and which no one else knows, until all is revealed.

So you recite your mantra. Do you really recite it, or are you like the parrot which makes the sound but can do no more? Are you *in* your mantra, or is the mantra half-hearted? Words can be said but not really meant. However, the true reciter communicates his or her self to the mantra so that the reciter and the recited are one. Truly to receive and truly to say the mantra means becoming the mantra, so that there is an identity of the sayer and the said.

This mantra or 'seed' of the Word informs the reciter's whole being and makes the reciter become the Word, so that the 'Word [is] made flesh' anew in the reciter's flesh.

The same point is true of the act of faith proclaimed at baptism. To say the name Jesus authentically is to form one body, one reality with Jesus. To truly say one's mantra means becoming the Mantra. To say one's word means becoming the Word.

It is possible to hold back from the mantra and use it only as a peg on which to hang a spirituality that is not naturally connected with the mantra. It is possible to use the mantra simply as a means to quieten the mind. In these cases the capacity of the mantra is scarcely used

By becoming one with the mantra, which has been received both by grace and from a tradition, the practitioner becomes one with the divine Mantra which is its source. The practitioner is 'transfigured into a copy' (Philippians 3:21) or expression of that divine Mantra. The reciter is recited once and for all by the One who dwells in silence. The reciter becomes eternal and acquires the state of the Word through whom all things were made and to whom all return, such that God is all in all.

5. Placing the mantra

'The words I have spoken to you are spirit and they are life.'
(John 6:63)

In the first instance, let it be noted that, because of the power of human touch, tactile therapies are increasingly used in modern medicine. Knotted muscles are untangled and the stresses of the mind are removed. To touch is to heal.

Furthermore, the body is a microcosm of the universe. The feet touch the earth while the head is linked to the sky. The heart is sensitive to the moods of the cosmos. The throat speaks the words that determine the use of the world's resources. The mind can contain the secrets of the universe. The body is not a machine but a complex of symbols.

Secondly, the mantra has all the power of the Mantra: 'The words I have spoken to you are spirit and they are life'. This is most powerfully seen in the consecration of bread and wine at Mass, when the words of Jesus are pronounced over the gifts so that they become Jesus himself. Their inmost reality is constituted by the words that have been said over them: 'This is my body; this is my blood'. The mantra used in meditation is not just a means of stabilising an over-active mind but is also a prophetic word, a powerful word of blessing.

When Jeremiah says in fright, 'Ah, Lord Yahweh: I am a child', God scolds him and says, 'There! I am putting my words into your mouth

… to destroy and overthrow, to build, and to plant' (Jeremiah 1:6, 10). Indeed, the mantra has the power of creating and recreating, of making a new heaven and a new earth, since through the Word 'all things came to be' (John:1.2).

Taking these two points together, it is understood why the bishop, at confirmation, should stretch out his hands and invoke wisdom, knowledge, counsel and reverence, and then touch the forehead of the candidate, which is the place of the 'third eye', the place of insight. By touching this point, the bishop activates it. He anoints it with chrism and projects the Holy Spirit into it.

Similarly, at baptism, the heart and the crown of the head are anointed; in the sacrament of healing, the forehead and the palms of the hand are anointed. In most of the sacraments there is an act of touching to purify and heal, to consecrate and empower.

To place the mantra on something is to change that thing into the mantra. To pronounce the sacred word over an object is to make that object sacred.

This act of the celebrant in the sacraments of confirmation and baptism can be imitated by the meditator. Although this point is not emphasized in the John Main tradition, which speaks only of the act of sitting, it is quite compatible as a preparatory exercise so that by blessing one spot the whole person should be blessed and in turn become a blessing to all.

The meditator may touch the eyebrow centre, so as to sensitize it, and then mentally places the mantra there at the zero point from which all proceeds, the place of wisdom and command. While there are many other centres that should eventually be activated, as will be shown later, this one is first empowered since all emotions and impulses function best when brought under the sway of wisdom.

The touch sensitizes the spot. The practitioner then recites the mantra placing it, so to speak, at the eyebrow centre. At the same time that the mantra is placed there, the respiration is imagined to be going through that spot so that the breath is felt to be entering and exiting there as a respiration. The mantra contains all the value and power of this tradition so that the centre is transubstantiated into the mantra. The eyebrow centre itself becomes the mantra.

The mantra is imparted to the eyebrow centre so that the human mind becomes the mind of God; the individual's authority is that of God himself. The communication of the mantra is the ultimate empowering.

However, the meditator may wish simply to charge the whole body, rather than some particular aspect, with the power of the mantra.

6. Mastering the mantra

'Those who sins you forgive they are forgiven; those whose sins you retain they are retained.' (John 20:22-23)

The mantra may have been given but it will remain ineffective if it is not used. Indeed, a significant period of practice is necessary for it to achieve its effects. A violinist, for example, may have musical talent, may indeed have a fine instrument and may have received excellent instruction, but many hours of practice are required if mastery is to be achieved. The violinist must become one with the instrument which then reflects the player's every mood while, conversely, the music hidden, so to speak, in the instrument inspires the violinist to play. The violinist masters the instrument only by becoming its servant. Any attempt to force will only cause a jarring sound. Similarly, the mastery of the mantra is not a control or domination but rather an expertise that comes from total integration of the reciter and the recited. Indeed the mantra inspires the reciter to recite just as much as the reciter has the ability naturally and effortlessly to recite the mantra. The reciter and the recited are one.

The Mantra

The violinist does not just play notes. The player, the instrument and the melody are one reality such that the question could be asked: is the violinist playing the violin or is the music so attractive that the violinist cannot help playing it? Or, again, does the instrument itself, because of its possibilities, inspire melody in the player? In the consummate artist all these are one.

There are two aspects to the mantra: the verbal form and the meaning given to it. The meditator who has been touched by grace has, indeed is, an aspect of the Word, and this aspect is imparted to the mantra. The verbal form of the mantra is imbued with meaning. The purpose of repeating the mantra is not only to acquire the habit of reciting it continually throughout the day but also to evoke one's charism continuously. In this way the mantra acquires all the power of the Mantra. The individual mantra becomes the expression of the practitioner's inmost being and has all the power of the inspiring Spirit. Thus the meditator, the gift of grace, the tradition and the mantra are one.

The mantra, like any spiritual gift, is not given for the practitioner alone nor is it given for just some other-worldly purpose. It is a word of power, of blessing, and a word of healing for the world. From it a resonance comes which fills the world. 'No utterance at all, no speech, no sound, that anyone can hear, yet their voice goes out through all the earth, and their message to the ends of the world' (Psalm 19:3-4). The practitioner, in reciting, senses that the mantra goes out like a clarion call to all the earth 'to destroy and overthrow, to build and to plant' (Jeremiah 1:10). The mantra, when mastered, is an instrument of mastery. The mantra is a means to bring the highest justice to bear in every situation so that good is restored and evil is removed. The world is thus ordered according to the truth of the mantra.

7. Speaking the mantra

*The man exclaimed: 'This at last is bone from my bones, and
flesh from my flesh. This is to be called woman, for this was
taken from man'. (Genesis 2:23)*

The mantra is a word, not just a sound repeated over and over. It is not a
word said to oneself, a sort of soliloquy. Nor is it just a distraction for the
mind so as to let the spirit soar. The mantra is an expression. It comes
from a tradition and expresses the tradition. It is received from the teacher,
as discussed earlier, who gives it to the disciple. It comes from the reciter
and expresses the reciter.

The mantra is the essence of the Word that surpasses all sound. The
mantra is an undertaking, for the mantra is not so much the vocable,
which is uttered with the lips or mind, but an attitude, an emotion, which
constitutes the essential self. By reciting the mantra the practitioner un-
dertakes to be true to his or her self.

Thus the mantra, like all words and expressions, is a bridge between the speaker and the one addressed. The mantra is necessarily said
to *someone*. I can become the mantra only if I say it to someone who
receives the mantra, who listens and accepts the mantra.

The mantra can be directed to the heavens and the earth and can
change things: 'You could say to this mountain: "Get up and throw yourself into the sea" and it would obey you' (Mark 11:23).

The mantra is a word, not of information but of covenant. The practitioner becomes the mantra for the sake of someone. It is recited for
someone and is said to someone. For the sake of whom? For whom does
the practitioner exist? To whom, above all, does the practitioner wish to
relate? Who best receives the meditator's word? Who is silent, present,
wanting to hear the practitioner's word and receiving the practitioner's

essence? Who draws the mantra from the reciter, inspiring it so that the reciter seems to sing a new song? Only the practitioner can give an answer to these questions.

According to the second account of creation in the Book of Genesis, when a helpmate was sought for the first man in his disturbing loneliness, all sorts of creatures are brought to him and he names them all, defining them and claiming them. But none of the creatures is adequate to the task. When, however, the woman is brought to him he exclaims, 'This at last is bone from my bone and flesh from my flesh'. The first biblical record of human speech is a marriage covenant.

The mantra can be said wholeheartedly only with respect to those who are loved, for love best arouses speech. The mantra is inspired by love and expresses love. Thus Jesus, the man for all seasons, is the Word addressed to all humankind, even to those who would not accept him.

The recitation of the mantra is often used in a private and intensely personal way. While this is valid it is not complete, for the word — and the mantra is supremely an expression of the Word — is always a communication, so that it is possible to recite the mantra with emphasis on its communication.

As it is, the teacher's recitation of the mantra in private is already a preparation for its bestowal on the disciple and, as already noted, the mantra is a word of blessing. It is possible, therefore, to say the mantra for those and to those who are loved. Therefore the practitioner first imagines someone with whom a loving relationship is enjoyed so the mantra is said in their regard. Then it is said to those personally unknown to the meditator but known by hearsay. Then, in an ever-increasing circle, the mantra is said to someone for whom hostility or resentment are felt. Then the mantra is said to the whole world, to all generations of people past and future, of every sort and condition.

8. Ending the mantra

'And when I am lifted up from the earth I shall draw all to myself.' (John 12:32)

All four evangelists mention the last utterance of Jesus on the cross. Luke and John give it as a sentence: 'Father, into your hands I commend my spirit' (Luke 23:46); and 'It is accomplished' (John 19:30). In Matthew and Mark it is simply a great cry, an exclamation, which constitutes the ultimate revelatory word.

The entry into the utter depth is at the same time entry into the fullness of life. Is it a cry of distress or of triumph? It is both, for on the cross humiliation and glory coincide. The last word has been said, after which there is silence.

The various aspects of the mantra have been noted: how it comes out of silence, how it is received, how it is begun, how the practitioner becomes the mantra, how it is placed, how it is used in consecration, how it is communicated, etc. Now we describe the end of the mantra, that comes from silence and enters into silence.

The word has been said, the work has been done: 'It is accomplished'. The recitation cannot be undone. The practitioner has acted under inspiration, for true recitation is given from above. The reciter has done what had to be done. There is a satisfaction at the end of the mantra.

Just as God performed the work of creation and, after judging that 'indeed it was very good' (Genesis. 1:31), rested on the seventh day, so too at the end of each recitation of the mantra there is a moment of rest, of gladness at the work well done. Indeed the practitioner should have the attitude that the mantra that is being said at any point in time is the last time the mantra will ever be said. In this way it will be well said.

Indeed it is true that one day the practitioner will no longer say a mantra. All temporal things will have come to an end in the repose of heaven itself.

At the end of the mantra, during those few moments when the breath stops and before it begins again, the practitioner becomes strongly aware of transcending the mantra, for the mantra comes to an end but the meditator continues. The practitioner's real character becomes evident, and the real mantra, which is the very self, becomes apparent.

The mantra has been recited and the work has been done, but the work in fact is not completely finished. The Eternal Silence says the Word once and forever; the Virgin Mary gives birth to the Word once and forever. But the practitioner is not so totally involved in the act of recitation so that the mantra must be repeated. At least there is a momentary rest at the end of the mantra

The Silence at the end of the mantra is not the same as the Silence at the beginning. The mantra comes out of Silence and is the expression of that Silence, but it is received into Silence as into virgin territory. The Silence at the end is an image of the Silence at the beginning but is not the same since the Silence from which the Word derives is different from the Silence into which it is received and in which it resonates. The first Silence is the source of the Mantra. The second Silence evokes the mantra. Which is more productive of sound: the Source or the Evocation? Thus the Transcendent One speaks the Word to the Holy Spirit — but that is another subject, rich and complex, to be handled at another time.

In short, the meditator focuses on the ending of the mantra, not at the end of the period of meditation but at the end of each saying of the mantra, at the moment when it finishes and before the next saying of it. In this way the meditator enters into restful silence.

9. All is mantra

*Sing the words and tunes of the psalms and hymns when you
are together and go on singing and chanting to the Lord in
your hearts, so that always and everywhere you are giving
thanks to God who is our Father ,in the name of our Lord Jesus
Christ. (Ephesians 5:20)*

From the fullness of Silence the Word is emitted which is yet of such a
quality that it reveals the Silence from whom it springs. The Speaker
speaks his only-begotten Son who reveals the Speaker. Silence evokes
the Word, and Silence receives the Word so that the Word suggests its
opposite. The Spirit inspires the eternal Son and listens fully to all the
Word is.

Thus the Silence is not an emptiness but a fullness. Rather it is both
empty and full, for it contains all that could be said. The Speaking Silence
is completely said in the Word. The Word, in turn, is said completely to
the Receiving Silence who is truly God evoking and receiving all that the
Speaking Silence can say. All this is true of the eternal Trinity and is true
of the mantra, which has a beginning and an end, a coming out of silence
and a moving into silence. Thus the recitation of the mantra is an image
of the Triune God.

The purpose of set times of prayer, however, is to transform all
time into prayer; the point of reciting the mantra is to turn all speech
into mantra. The 'mantrist', the reciter of the mantra, does not want to
divide life into times of prayer and times of non-prayer, into the sacred
and the profane, but rather seeks to 'pray at all times', so that every act
becomes ritual and every word becomes a mantra.

It is not a question of thinking about prayer all day long. It is a
matter of allowing the time of meditation quite spontaneously to influ-

ence the whole day. The practitioner who comes to deep rest in meditation spreads that restfulness beyond the formal time of prayer. The more
the mantra is imbued with the Mantra, the more everyday words will be
suffused by the Mantra.

Furthermore, having in the most profound sense become the Word,
the practitioner's whole world is also transfigured into the Word.

Indeed, the whole point of the set time of meditation is, surprisingly, to put an end to the time of meditation. When all is mantra and all
is meditation, there is no difference between the allotted hour and the
rest of the day. If every word is the Word and every act is worship, if God
is present in every moment and the reciter is present to the Holy One in
all relationships, is not the practitioner both in heaven and on earth? Has
not the kingdom come?

In fact the future of humanity lies in that direction: when earth
becomes heaven and heaven becomes earth. Equally, all words and deeds
will manifest the Silence and be addressed to the Silence. A great hush
will descend upon the world, the work will be done, and all will be at
rest.

HEARING

1. Opening the Book

The Book of the genealogy of Jesus Christ (Matthew 1:1)

The Book is placed on the table. What secrets does it contain, what threats or promises, for it has come down through the centuries and contains in a few pages the wisdom revealed over millennia? It lies there, awesome and wonderful, closed.

The opening of the Book is a gesture of revelation. What was closed is now opened, what was hidden is now revealed. It is 'gospel', 'good news', a consolation, a promise of hope, a message, a summons, a source of power.

It has been transmitted from generation to generation, cherished and handed down. It is a gift from the church to the church, but above all it is from above, a gift revealing the Giver.

The first words are a great clarion call: 'The Book of the genealogy of Jesus Christ'. From the outset the good news is Jesus of Nazareth, the Christ. All the words that follow are the unfolding of that one Word, spoken once and forever from all eternity.

Each word of the gospels is a mantra, making and remaking the world. All words lead back to the one Word. The purpose of the stories and sayings of the gospels is to take the reader to the Silence. The reader then becomes the Word, both vibrant and still.

The Silence speaks the Word who is made manifest in the words printed on the page, which in turn allow the disciple to become the Word and so know the Silence. This is the great cycle: leading from the Silence to the printed letter and back to the Silence.

In this meditation, the practitioner sits in silent appreciation before the Book and is taken by it to the Word made flesh and so into the Silence of the One who speaks.

2. Hearing the Gospel

'Listen, anyone who has ears.' (Matthew 13:9)

The babble of competing desires is deafening. The words of the gospel may indeed be spoken but the recipient may not hear. There must first be a quieting of the mind and an opening of the heart by the grace of the Spirit. No one can hear the words of the gospel and discern their true meaning without inspiration. The Spirit who inspires the written words inspires their hearing. The Spirit hovers at the very beginning of the process of hearing the gospel.

The Word, uttered once and forever from Silence, must be heard in silence. This involves a radical poverty of spirit so that nothing stands in the way. It involves a relaxation of heart and an emptying of mind. It implies a readiness to hear whatever comes and a willingness to undertake whatever is commanded. It means abandoning all control and every ambition, placing no conditions, becoming the obedient disciple, ready for all and expecting nothing. Thus the Spirit makes the field fertile, able to produce a harvest, thirty, sixty, one hundred fold.

Mary of Nazareth had no formal education yet understood the meaning of the Sacred Writings. Though without academic understanding of the text she appreciated its significance, which penetrated into her soul and prepared her to give flesh to the Word.

Thus, the first attitude in meditative listening is to enter into silence and to accept whatever comes. It is a radical discipleship.

3. Closing the Book

Jesus then rolled up the scroll . . . Then he began to speak to them, 'This text is being fulfilled today even as you listen'. (Luke 4:20-21)

The Word comes out of Silence and leads into Silence. It arises from the heart and is heard in the heart — 'As for Mary, she treasured all these things and pondered them in her heart' (Luke 2:19). If the Word does not arise from the heart it is less than total and if it does not lodge in the heart it is wasted.

Those who hear the Word of God become the Word. The closing of the printed book shows that the Gospel has come to stay. It is the second coming of the Word.

The highest acclaim of the Word is the silence where all questions have been resolved and a great stillness descends. The Gospel leads beyond sound and repetition to the one Word said once and forever.

So the Book of the Gospels is at last closed, not finished but fulfilled. It is not read any more because it has been heard. All thought has come to an end because the meditator has arrived at knowledge. There is the great Silence, full of resonance, unstruck, humming and vibrating, delicate and overwhelming, unabating and never tiresome. Sound submits to Silence so that in the end Silence reigns.

Hearing

There is ecstasy both in the One who has expressed the Word of love and in the disciple who has heard the Word of love. Both are outside themselves in love.

The Breath

1. Inhalation

*Yahweh God fashioned the man of dust from the soil. Then he
breathed into his nostrils a breath of life, And thus the man
became a living being. (Genesis 2:7)*

In the cycle of breathing, the transition between exhalation and inhalation is particularly noteworthy. There is in fact a somewhat lengthy pause, one or two seconds, between the moment of exhalation and the moment of inhalation, a moment of quiet and inactivity. (By contrast, there is virtually no pause between the end of the inhalation and beginning of the exhalation.) During inspiration the breath enters the nostrils and oxygen penetrates into the body with its intoxicating vigour. It is a moment of pleasure, for life is felt to move within. The practitioner rejoices in this life and says 'yes' to it, welcoming it and receiving it, for the attitude to breathing is a measure of the attitude to life. Indeed, respiration can be anxious and shallow, or easy and full, depending on the situation. Character is revealed in the breathing patterns.

In meditation, the meditator can focus on the breathing, the natural function that occurs more than 20,000 times each day, from the moment of birth till the dying breath. It is interesting to note that in the

Indian tradition respiration is called a recitation (*japa*) and is considered to be a form of mantra meditation. In fact, respiration is called a 'natural' (*sahaja*) recitation, and a 'recitation without a mantra' (*ajapa-japa*) that seems to echo the sounds *sa* (during inhalation) and *ham* (during exhalation). In this view it is possible to perform recitation without a vocal mantra.

The respiration should be conscious. Indeed, a major purpose of breath control (*pranayama*) in yoga is to make breathing a conscious act: natural yet deliberate, not subject to passions such as resentment or craving but in accord with the untrammelled mind, enjoyed but not craved. Respiration ceases to be just automatic, for the practitioner is truly breathing, fully aware, enjoying the breath. There is no reflection, no thinking, no interpretation, no theologising, but just the welcoming experience of breath. And as a result the system is cleansed, the whole being is invigorated, indeed inspired. 'The man became a living being.'

The transition between expiration and inspiration encapsulates the whole of life — inhalation recapitulates the first breath taken on being born into this world and every human being shall one day expire and in the exhalation that last moment is anticipated. Life and death are expressed in that moment of transition. Life is to be welcomed and death is to be accepted. Thus the meditator's attitude to that moment of transition influences the attitude to life as a whole.

2. Inspiration

The life and death of each of us has its effect on others.
(Romans 14:7)

Breath has never been understood to mean just the inhalation of oxygen and the exhalation of carbon dioxide. This is because the emotions and the interior life are revealed in the breath. For example, a place has 'atmosphere', one person may be a bit 'stuffy' while another is 'like a breath of fresh air". The effect of one on another each other is symbolized by breath.

Mary, the mother of Jesus, who stood nearest the cross, received into her lungs the last breath of Jesus and so is the first to receive his redeeming Spirit. On the day of Easter, Jesus stands among the disciples gathered in the room and breathes on them, saying, 'Receive the Holy Spirit' (John 20:22). And again, on Pentecost Day, when they are gathered in the one room they hear the sound of a mighty wind and are filled with the Holy Sprit and begin to proclaim the Christian mantras (Acts 2:1).

The breath of Jesus moves in the community of the Church and amongst those gathered in meditation where the vitality, the breath, of each person impinges on the other and facilitates meditation. The practitioners sense this influence as they breathe in each other's life and breathe out their life for others. It means assenting to the truth within and acknowledging that a Breath is shared that surpasses the sum total of breaths. The meditators acknowledge that the Breath has been imparted to the church and indeed to the whole world. They acknowledge a higher, more expansive Breath and to this Breath assent is given so that the lungs expand to receive it, for it is the saving Breath, the inspiring, invigorating Breath, cleansing and healing.

As a result a calm develops and the natural breath becomes very relaxed. These are signs of a deeper event occurring beyond knowledge in the depths where the divine Spirit meets the human spirit (I Corinthians 2:11).

3. The Spirit

'What is born of the Spirit is spirit.' John 3:6

The Holy Spirit is the Third Person of the Blessed Trinity and is God. The Spirit overshadowed Mary so that she conceived the Word; the Spirit came down on Jesus like a dove at his baptism in the Jordan; and by the power of the Spirit he was raised from the dead. The Spirit given by the Father to Jesus is sent by Jesus from the Father to the church. This is the Gift of the Father to the Son, the word of blessing, the approval inhabiting the Word as he offers praise to the Father.

The Divine Author sees the Son, who is the perfect expression of his being and out of love for him gives him the Spirit whom the Author also loves and who is like a window opening out onto infinite worlds of possibility. In the power of the Spirit the Son is active. At the sight of the Spirit, the Son senses his freedom in ways unknown before, and knows an overwhelming sense of joy he had not yet experienced. The Spirit inspires the Son, perfect expression though he is of the Inexpressible.

How can that theology be used in meditation on the breath? The breath is a most powerful symbol of the Holy Spirit. Indeed, the very word 'spirit' means 'breath'. Every meditation on the breath eventually leads to an experience of the Spirit, just as meditation on the mantra leads to a knowledge of the Word. And since, of course, Word and Spirit are essentially related and mutually involved, meditation on the breath leads to an experience of the Word just as meditation on the mantra eventually leads to the fullness of the Spirit.

The ultimate and greatest act is to breathe forth the Holy Spirit. The church which receives the Holy Spirit into its lungs at Pentecost breathes forth the Holy Spirit upon the world and so becomes one Body in Christ, one Spirit in the Spirit. 'What is born of the Spirit is spirit,' what is Spirit makes Spirit.

The meditator breathes forth not just ordinary breath but also the fire of the Spirit. With this knowledge the meditator senses the freedom, the vitality, the inspiration and the joy that is within.

The practitioner breathes from the heart, imparting the breath and its power to the centre of the forehead, as though there were a pipe between the furnace in the heart and the eyebrow centre, transforming it by the power of the Spirit, so that all becomes Spirit.

Then, from the heart and from the place of insight and wisdom, of right judgment and fortitude between the eyebrows, the Spirit is imparted to others so that the Spirit, like tongues of fire, comes to rest on each other's head in a new Pentecost.

The Body

In the experienced meditator, all the faculties and aspects of the body are involved since the human being is physical; meditation is a bodily act as much as spiritual and mental. All the centres are to be open if meditation is to occur with full involvement and without distraction.

However, there may be value in emphasising one or other of the various centres if they have become dormant. The body is like a flute, and the different centres are like the finger-holes: when all are open the melody can be played.

The eight chakras

The Sanskrit word *chakra* simply means a wheel. (The correct spelling is *cakra*, with the 'c' pronounced 'ch'; thus it is more usually written 'chakra'.) Since a wheel consists of hub, spokes and outer rim, *chakra* can also mean radiation from a centre or, conversely, a vortex that draws everything to itself. It can also refer to a discus, the weapon used in battle, or to the circular blade, which cuts deep. It can refer to a group of things or a group of people united in a common purpose. Thus the word 'chakra' has a dynamic sense: it is a radiance or a vortex; it cuts, creates, it opens and joins.

By further extension the word also refers to various centres in the body, which powerfully influence thoughts and feelings. To affect these is to bring about fundamental changes in perception and action.

It must also be noted, as of first importance, that the wheel has a void at its centre — the hub. If this is obstructed the wheel cannot turn. The dynamism of the chakra depends, therefore, on the void, the stillness, at its centre.

The word 'mantra', in the Indian thought system, has an instrumental sense. The first syllable 'man' refers to the mind (*manas*) while the second syllable 'tra' has an operative sense. As a spade is an instrument in the hand, the mantra is an instrument of the mind, designed to produce an effect.

> Yes, as the rain and the snow come down from the heavens and do not return without watering the earth, making it yield and giving growth to provide seed for the sower and bread for the eating, so the word that goes from my mouth does not return to me empty, without carrying out my will and succeeding in what it was sent to do. (Isaiah 55:10-11)

Therefore, the mantra is not just a means of distracting oneself from distracting thoughts. It is an authoritative word, an inspired word that heals and empowers, for it is a version of the Word through whom and for whom all things are made. Likewise the breath is a symbol of the Spirit and as such can sanctify and empower, regenerate and transform.

From all these considerations, its follows that mantra and breath can be placed on the chakras.

The model for this act is provided, in fact, by the sacraments of the Church, notably the sacrament of Confirmation when the bishop anoints the forehead at Confirmation. He chooses that spot precisely because it is naturally disposed to the gifts of the Spirit. It is by nature the place of 'wisdom and insight, counsel and power, knowledge and reverence' (Isaiah 11:2). The bishop seals the place with the Spirit because the Spirit is already present there in some way. If the Spirit did not already invite, the Spirit could not be received. By virtue of the Spirit, that place is open to the Spirit. Spirit welcomes Spirit.

This placement can be done personally by the practitioner in times of private meditation. It can be done by the authorized leader in times of group meditation, or even by intention when others are absent.

Although various considerations will be made concerning each of the chakras, the meditator simply focuses on the relevant chakra without thinking over any of these points. The chakra is blessed by breath and mantra.

The third eye

In the series of acts described in what follows, the first centre to be blessed is between the eyebrows, the 'third eye', the symbol of insight.

The meditator understands the eyebrow centre as a radiance or vortex of energies. Actually touching this place can help sensitize it. Then with full confidence, indeed with the power of the Spirit and in union with the Word made flesh, the mantra and the breath are imparted.

The place has been marked by the Spirit and takes on the character of the Spirit, a freedom beyond words, real but intangible, beyond time, spacious, open, and wide as the sea. The Spirit who hovers over the deep at the very origin (Genesis 1.1) and who, in the end, calls out with the Bride, 'Come Lord Jesus' (Revelations 22:17), the same Spirit is located at the place of the 'third eye', the eye of perception which sees beyond the visible to what no one has seen or imagined, 'things beyond the human mind' (1 Corinthians 2:9).

Indeed, surprisingly, the breath of the Spirit seems to be felt at this point, moving freely in and out as though through an opening , not forced, full of peace, pleasurable, enjoyable. There may also be a slight contraction, which occurs naturally, as though wishing to feel the friction of the breath more intently.

From the centre, like spokes from a wheel, the energies move in and out, as so many gifts: wisdom, counsel, right judgment, reverence, awe and wonder. The practitioner allows the energy to radiate from that point into the very centre of the head where the pituitary gland is located, the gland which governs all the others. In time the energy of the Spirit flows into the whole person, bringing tranquility and balance, strength and energy to every part of the body.

A great calm and sense of stability develops, a sense of authority and strength — indeed all the gifts of the Spirit start to manifest themselves. There is an increase in wisdom and a growing reverence for all things. The conflicting passions are put to rest and an equanimity results, which copes with both good and bad knowing that the transcending Spirit overcomes all obstacles. The strength of a good conscience gives vigour and assurance. Sight becomes clear and the eyes acquire a lustre and a penetration because they see beyond the perceptible. The eye of faith opens further and things unseen become evident. In fact, so wonderful is the sight that glamour holds little attraction and the inner quality of things becomes apparent.

It is recommended that a definite level of experience be attained at the eyebrow centre. This place of insight and wisdom, of authority and reverence, provides a suitable guide for the power, which will become apparent in the other centres.

The first chakra (mūladhāra)
The perineum

The first chakra is located at the base of the body, at what is called the 'perineum' or 'the pelvic floor' and consists of a criss-cross of muscles located between the anus and the sex organ.

The first chakra is the place of the hidden coil where all the energies are present in unmanifest form. The so-called *kundalini*, which in Sanskrit means a 'ring', lies here like a coiled serpent. It is the place of the Spirit, the rock from which the waters of grace flow, the place of faith.

This root chakra is imagined as square and ochre coloured, a solid base associated with the earth, for it is where people sit. It is the place of connection with the ground and all its forces. The rock rests immobile, and quiet. So too the meditator sits solid as a rock, not tense but firm, not loose but compact, content simply to be there. Just as the rock is inert, the meditator accepts to be of earth, of this time and place, real and stable. Just as the rock is quiet, the meditator too is not engaged in thought, for faith is an awareness deeper than thought. There is nothing spectacular about meditation except that the meditator is led to it by grace. Indeed, a person cannot sit still in meditation unless they are led to that spot.

On the rock of Peter's faith the whole structure of the church has been built. The meditator likewise sits in faith, secure in the hidden, inarticulate knowledge that first comes from grace. To sit quietly is to have faith; to be restless and vacillating is to lack trust.

Not only is the body stable but the mind too becomes quiet; the fluctuating emotions and the changing thoughts become still. The meditator can then go into the depths, beneath the ego, the desires and the fears, arriving at the essential truth. It is the place of honesty and humility.

By silence and stillness the meditator comes to the real self and senses the gift that has been imparted. It is the point where the depths of the spirit meet the depths of the divine Spirit. It is the deep spring from which the fountain of life (John 4:14) springs up.

Moses struck the rock and out gushed the water (Numbers 20:11), giving life to the Israelites and their cattle. The meditator focuses on the rock-like base of his or her being and strikes it, not with a staff but with breath and mantra. With each exhalation and recitation, this place is struck, not harshly but confidently, with assurance and not hesitating like Moses who did not enter the Promised Land because of his doubt. The place is struck with the knowledge that water will indeed flow and irrigate all the other charkas, making them function, each in turn. All this is possible only with faith.

In this way the meditator becomes a quiet rock of faith at the deepest level of being symbolized by the base of the body. The focus is therefore brought to the centre of the seat, the pelvic floor, or perineum. It may help to contract the pelvic floor slightly in order to feel where this point is. To focus on this area is to acknowledge one's physicality, one's limitation in this time and place; it means coming to the ground of one's being, to the depths of one's spirit.

The meditator eventually acquires a great stability of character and becomes a dependable rock of faith. Then the Spirit will be felt to arise from that point and make a journey through all the other chakras to reach above the head, the meeting point of heaven and earth. It is a journey all must make.

The spot may start to vibrate and throb, and from it energy will arise and fill the whole body. This throbbing is to be noted and allowed. It is a sign and is to be welcomed but not sought. What counts is the faith that led to the breaking open of the fountain and the effects that flow.

This journey is a growth in consciousness whereby the practitioner comes to the fullness of the Truth. For some this growth is accompanied by spectacular displays of intense emotion, blinding light, etc. What counts, however, is the growth itself, which may occur in an unspectacular way. Indeed, greater importance attaches to the unspectacular than to the spectacular.

The second chakra (svādhisthāna)
The sexual organ

The second chakra is located at the sexual organ. As with all the chakras, its location is not very precise for it is not so much an anatomical spot as a reservoir of energies, both emotional and spiritual, a symbolic and experiential centre, which can vary in location from individual to individual.

The lap is where children love to climb and nestle. Icons of Mary show her holding the Child on her lap as on a throne, presenting the Saviour to whom she has given birth. It is the place of blessing and fruitfulness. 'Give and there will be gifts for you. A full measure, pressed down, shaken together and running over, will be poured into your lap' (Luke 6:38).

We are all born of the union of male and female. This is God's creative process from which all life springs forth. It deserves the highest respect.

The sexual organ is also closely tied to the subconscious that is perhaps even more revealing than the conscious level. In Sanskrit it is called 'the place of the self' *(svādhisthāna)*, for the impressions of childhood and of family, of culture and tradition, are stored there and passed on to the next generation. Mental impressions and the lives of forbears leave their traces there; the fundamentally painful and pleasant experiences are held there. The sense of essential personality is lodged there.

The sexual organ and its significance are too frequently passed over in spiritual discourse and this neglect is damaging since all chakras need to be acknowledged and given their rightful role both in public and in private. The centres of the human psyche are brought into right balance when they are recognized with calm openness.

The purpose of meditating on this chakra is to acknowledge and assent to it, to bless it and give thanks for it. The pure light of conscious thanksgiving has 'healing in its rays' (Malachi 3:20) and can eventually heal any disturbance that might have occurred there. The blessing of grace empowers and vitalizes this important dimension of our being and allows the vitality of faith to become manifest.

If the base of the body is associated with faith, which is the start of the spiritual journey, the lap, the 'place of the self', is associated with the outflow of water which springs from the rock of Peter's faith, in other words with the impetus and vitality of faith which leads to all sorts of fruitfulness.

Accordingly, the method of this meditation is to focus the attention on that place by means of the mantra and the breathing and so both heal it and bless it.

The third chakra (maṇipūra)
The solar plexus

The third chakra is located in the navel and is concerned above all with decision. Popular language shows this well. People speak of someone having 'guts', meaning that they have courage; or of a person being 'yellow bellied', meaning that they are cowardly. People experience 'butterflies in the stomach' when they are unsure. Someone may 'have no stomach' for an action which they do not wish to perform. By contrast, people talk of someone having 'fire in the belly', meaning that they are determined on some course of action.

From here we take our sustenance from the food we eat and translate it into the energy of creative activity.

The stomach is the place of the will where the impetus of grace becomes decisive, chosen. If the impetus experienced at the second chakra is not made decisive at the third it becomes dissipated and ineffectual.

On the other hand if the decision is not spontaneous and instinctual it is shown to be forced.

The fourth chakra (anāhata)
The heart

The heart is the place of the emotions, as when someone is described as 'warm-hearted' or 'cold-hearted'. Indeed there is a whole vocabulary of the heart, for it is the place of relationships. Furthermore, it can refer to the very centre from which all derives — the 'heart of the matter' — and to the place of mystery — the 'cave of the heart'.

It is at once at the centre of one's being and expansive. It balances the other chakras. The open heart is welcoming and spacious, all-encompassing like the air which gives life to all creatures. When it is open it refines and uplifts the energies of the other centres. It is the place of love, where the decisive choice becomes heartfelt, natural and human; and indeed it is the gateway to the divine heart. If the decision is not heartfelt it becomes inflexible and regardless. If the emotion of love is not based on decision it is vapid.

The heart involves the whole being and the whole being leads to the heart. Love springs from the deepest level of one's being, or else it will not last. If there is no emotional component, love will be unconvincing. All the chakras must come into play in their due order if a person is to love adequately. If one of them is paralysed, commitment will not be whole and lasting.

The fifth chakra (viśuddhi)
The throat

From the heart, the energy moves to the throat and so to speech, for it is natural that the heart should declare itself. This fact is shown by ordinary language. A person may 'speak from the heart' or 'cry from the heart'. There is relief in 'getting it off the chest'. And a person who speaks from the heart 'speaks freely'. The words are projected into space. The act of faith, which justifies a person, is a profession made from the heart (Romans 10:10). The love a person has for another is revealed and confirmed in speech. By contrast deceit is a dislocation between heart and speech.

Thus the fifth chakra is called *viśuddhi*, 'purification', 'clarification'. It is the chakra of revelation and purification.

The sixth chakra (*ājñā*)
Between the eyebrows

The sixth chakra, as we have already seen, is the place of insight, authority and command *(ājñā)*. It shows the practical outcome of the act of faith. Thus St Paul speaks that those who are spiritual have the right to assess the value of everything (1 Corinthians 2:15), and to bring justice to bear.

Only by truthfully declaring one's conviction can a person gain credibility and authority. By contrast, deceit and obfuscation destroy a person's right to lead.

The seventh chakra (*sahasrāra*)
The crown of the head

The seventh chakra is on the crown of the head, where a lotus of a thousand petals *(sahasrāra)* is imagined to reside. The natural authority of the true leader is acknowledged by the act of crowning, or its equivalent. On the crown of the head the ancient priests and kings and prophets were anointed with chrism, as still happens in the baptism of infants. In the ordination of bishops the celebrants' hands are extended over the head to symbolize the descent of the Holy Spirit coming from heaven. It is the transition point between earth, as symbolized by the body, and heaven, as symbolized by the space above.

To meditate on this chakra is to make the bridge between heaven and earth. The practitioner who has developed this chakra 'walks tall' and is not bowed down by the troubles of life.

The eighth chakra (dvādaśānta)
Above the head

The eighth chakra — according to some traditions such as the teaching of Kashmir Shaivism — is located some twelve finger-widths above *(dvādaśānta)* the head. It is the place where, in the portrayal of the baptism of the Lord, the Spirit is depicted as hovering. It is the place where the Spirit, the gift of the Most High, dwells.

It is the counterpart of the first chakra and is its 'octave', so to speak. When the Spirit has made the journey, from the lowest chakra at the very base of one's being to the highest chakra above one's head, then complete fulfilment has been attained. All power in heaven and on earth has been given. The fullness of heavenly and earthly joy is experienced: transcendence and immanence are one.

The whole journey

The base chakra contains in hidden form the whole prospective journey. By grace, this reserve is opened and the waters of life begin to flow and to be experienced profoundly in the region of the second chakra. Again by grace, the essential defining charism is affirmed at the symbolic level of the third chakra. All these things are brought into harmony and full-ness, into truth and love, again by grace, at the heart. The secret of the heart is declared, under the impact of grace, in the throat and put into action under the guidance of right judgment which is deeply felt at the forehead. The justification of the journey is experienced more power-fully at the crown of the head and leads to the sense of wholeness and holiness symbolically located above the head, at the place of the sacred nimbus.

Put simply, the journey of faith starts from the base and leads up-wards: what was hidden is fully revealed. The end is in the beginning. The higher chakras do not eliminate the lower but manifest them and bring them to fulfilment.

The practitioner may focus on one or other chakra so as to reinforce or heal it, but when all the various stages and aspects are har-monized the meditator enters into deep prayer.

PART II

This second section explores mantra-meditation in a different way. It shows how this form of meditation can be intimately associated with the events of sacred history and with the seasons of the church year. Mantra-meditation deepens the appreciation of the events and seasons, and conversely the celebration of these events heightens the significance of the meditative act.

ADVENT

1. The departure

Now at this time Caesar Augustus issued a decree for a census of the whole world to be taken. This census — the first — took place while Quirinius was governor of Syria, and everyone went to his own town to be registered. So Joseph set out from the town of Nazareth in Galilee and travelled up to Judea, to the town of David called Bethlehem, since he was of David's House and line, in order to be registered together with Mary, his betrothed, who was with child. (Luke 2:1-5)

Joseph sets out from Galilee, leaving all that is familiar to him in order to journey to his home town, Bethlehem, which he does not know. Yet it is a homecoming, for he is from the house and line of David. The journey is of interest not because it happened once but because it happens each time on entry into meditation, for meditation is the homecoming, the journey to the place of true belonging, to the cave of the heart, the manger.

But Joseph's journey is not easy for it involves a long walk on foot from Nazareth to Bethlehem, the whole length of the Holy Land. He retraces the whole of Israel's history. Likewise, the practitioner who takes up the meditative posture has already accomplished a long journey, with all its pitfalls, its highs and lows.

Joseph leaves Nazareth and travels night and day simply because the Emperor has ordered a census, which in Jewish eyes (2 Samuel 24:10) is sinful. Yet, this unjust decree is used by God so that the Messiah comes to be born in the city of David. So too in meditation the practitioner leaves all else behind and steps out into the unknown. Acknowledging the strange acts of God, who uses faults, illnesses, even sins, to achieve the divine purpose, the practitioner accepts all the light and shade of life, the hidden, shameful things, and moves on. The tears just beneath the surface are shed and left behind. The meditator presses on into the future hardly knowing what is in store.

Joseph travels with Mary, his betrothed, who is with child. As she walks, or perhaps rides on a donkey, the child in her is growing and moving. Similarly, from the outset the Word inhabits the meditator and comes to birth within. The meditator too is pregnant with hope, leaving all that is familiar, moving into the unknown, aware by faith that the Word is being formed from within, confident of the future.

2. The birth

While they were there the time came for her to have her child, and she gave birth to a son, her first-born. She wrapped him in swaddling clothes, and laid him in a manger because there was no room for them at the inn. (Luke 2:6-7)

Joseph and Mary have left Nazareth and set out for Bethlehem. Likewise, the first stage of meditation, occurring under the inspiration of the Spirit, requires the meditator to leave all that is familiar and to set out into the unknown, which is yet the place of origin, the homeland.

It is there that the time came for Mary to have her child. So too in meditation, at a time beyond human choosing, the Word is born. An attitude of expectancy and waiting is needed. In place of knowledge and wilfulness, the practitioner hearkens to Someone greater.

Then, by the grace of God, the Word is born. Similarly, in the quiet of meditation the Mantra arises that is not some sound that could be pronounced or adequately described. This is the crucial point. When everything has been stripped away, the inner self becomes evident. The true self, born from above, becomes apparent. Although the mantra given by a spiritual tradition continues to be recited, it now acquires its inner substance and nature. The word becomes the Word.

The practice of the mantra means becoming aware of the true Self and refashioning the whole of life. The meditator is refashioned according to the Word that has transformed the mantra. The focus is on the Word who inspires the mantra rather than on the mantra itself.

Mary takes the child and wraps him in swaddling clothes and lays him in a manger. She gives the signs indicating what sort of Messiah he is. She has not brought into the world a mighty warrior but a baby. She wraps him in swaddling clothes just as one day he will be wrapped in a shroud. She places him in the eating trough, because he is to be food for all humanity.

Likewise the mantra which arises from within has all the power of the Almighty. To receive the mantra and so become the mantra means setting all else aside. The mantra is a source of spiritual nourishment and a restorative. The centre of life has been found.

There was no room in the inn. The stable is famous, the inn is not. The supposed site of the stable is a place of pilgrimage; the inn is forgotten.

Only those situations and modes of conduct which lead to the arising of the second, the real, mantra, will be revisited and blessed.

3. The good news

In the countryside close by there were shepherds who lived in
the fields and took it in turns to watch their flocks during the
night. The angel of the Lord appeared to them and the glory of
the Lord shone round them. They were terrified, but the angel
said, 'Do not be afraid. Listen, I bring you news of great joy, a
joy to be shared by the whole people. Today in the town of
David a saviour has been born to you; he is Christ the Lord'.
(Luke 2:8-12)

The shepherds lie awake in the dark of night; indeed the whole people
of Israel are held in darkness, for no prophet had appeared since
Zechariah.

The term 'mantra' can be considered from without and from within.
The exterior mantra is recited but the interior mantra is an attitude of
heart. The recited mantra is influenced by the measure of grace that has
been received. When the real mantra appears it becomes clear how much
life has been lived in ignorance, unaware of the true Word at the heart of
things.

The shepherds are shaken at the appearance of the angel. They are
filled with awe and uncertainty at the irruption of the uncontrollable
God into their lives. Likewise, when the mantra begins to be perceived,
there is a wonderful fear. Indeed, if there is no real fear there is no real
mantra.

The angel says to all, 'Do not be afraid', lest the apparition be mis-
understood. So too at first the interior mantra can be puzzling and per-
turbing, especially if, like the birth of the Child, it differs from the attitudes of those who are respected mentors.

The birth of Jesus in Bethlehem is reflected in the interior birth of the Word. Meditation is Christmas in the life of the meditator. Christmas does not happen just once but happens whenever the Word is made manifest.

The angel announces the good news: 'Today, in the city of David, a saviour has been born for you'. The shepherds understand that the child is the Christ, and they are filled with joy. Similarly when the interior mantra is understood to be a word from above, a saving, powerful word given freely, joy floods out. 'Behold I bring you news of great joy to be shared by all the people.' The Word made flesh in the stable is worshipped as is the divine Mantra communicated in meditation.

4. The homecoming

And suddenly with the angel there was a great throng of the
heavenly host, praising God and singing:
'Glory to God in highest heaven, and peace to those who enjoy
his favour'. (Luke 2:13-14)

After leaving Nazareth, after being banned from the inn, after the fall of night and after the shock at the presence of the angel, all gather together in peace: Mary, Joseph, the Child, the shepherds, and even, according to legend, the ox and the donkey. Heaven and earth are united in peace and exultation.

The scene is profoundly moving for it reveals the essential nature of things. There is at the heart of things a peace and a joy that the bother of life and sheer ignorance mask from view. The purpose of meditation is to arrive at this peace and to enter into the silent stillness of the stable. By coming to the crib we come to ourselves, and by drawing close to the Christ Child we draw close to our own self.

The stable is the counterpart of the cross. In the one case there is hushed joy, in the other the depth of suffering. Yet in both cases limitation gives way to the peace that is the secret of the universe.

In meditation words give way to hushed silence at the Word made flesh and the calm of the Firstborn is experienced in the meditative posture. This tranquillity is accompanied by an expansive glory filling heaven and earth, and by peace flooding out from the crib to all humankind. In this way all are taken up into the wonder of the Word made flesh. It is the homecoming.

CHRISTMASTIDE

1. The infant

The newborn lies in the manger. No thought disturbs the sleep. His is a state of trust and confidence, security and hope. All is present in him, like the great banyan tree that exists potentially in its seed. All knowledge, the whole future, all the eventual acts and words are present in the child. After the dramatic process of birth the infant rests, a fact on the face of the earth, the source of salvation. Whatever will be known is already there, just as any shape is possible in the unformed clay.

By contemplating the baby, the meditator is drawn into silence and intimacy. The meditator is taken by the Spirit and united with the infant. The Spirit has full sway, imparting an attitude of trust and assurance, without fear or ambition, without craving or obduracy. The meditator is led to the state before thought and choice, where every option is available, a state of openness and acceptance and infinite possibility. It is cleansing because it is a return to the foundational innocence.

Thus the meditator relives and recapitulates the experience of the newborn Christ, rediscovering the state of the infant, which is not a position of impotence but of potentiality. Indeed, it is a position of authority for everything springs from the God-Infant. Already as he lies in the crib his lips begin to formulate the words that will resonate through the ages, and his limbs prepare to bless and heal.

The meditator experiences and takes on the state of the infant in the manger who has attracted countless numbers to his crib. It is the moment of converting and becoming like the little children who alone inherit the kingdom of heaven.

2. The child

Time passes. The newborn child is the seed sown on the face of the earth, containing in essence all that will be said of himself by himself.

Spontaneously and naturally he begins to stir and open his eyes; his mind begins to observe and organize the impressions that flood in. The light of his intelligence observes all around him and begins to comprehend and eventually to speak. It is the time of infancy.

The meditator who enters into the silence, drawn there by the newborn Word, returns to a pre-cognitive stage. Even if thoughts and distractions jump around in the mind, the heart is elsewhere and gradually begins to perceive the movements of the Spirit and to understand.

Two contrasting events occur during the infancy. On the one hand magi from the East suddenly appear and, finding Jesus seated on Mary's lap, offer him tribute of gold, frankincense and myrrh. He perceives, with all the impressionability and incomprehension of childhood, their worshipping amazement. On the other hand, Jesus and Mary are taken at dead of night in headlong escape from Herod's soldiers. Thus, in some incoherent and inchoate way, he knows acclamation and hate, wealth and deprivation, security and vulnerability. Indeed, all children know extremes of fear and love.

The practitioner, in the various experiences of meditation, begins to select those elements that suit the Word within, accepting what is true and rejecting what is false so that wisdom is acquired. False truths are exposed, while the time of testing is seen as valuable. The meditator learns to name the experiences and to assess their worth. By the reactions of the Spirit the meditator begins to appreciate the essential character and to know the true self.

Well before the child Jesus can understand and express himself, he has the essential insight into his own being. Although he needs to learn a language and a culture, and to have his character formed by social contact and the traditions of his people, he has that insight, which grows in clarity and stability as he acquires the tools to express it. His self is given from the start; his self-knowledge comes gradually. He has insight into himself well before he knows he has insight. Only with time will he have clarity enough to publicly state the knowledge he has acquired.

The meditator goes through the same stages, moving from the Word which they have become, and progressing through insight into their nature, to a hesitant verbalization of what they are, and finally to pro-claiming it openly, coming, at last, to sing a new song.

3. The adolescent

The years pass. The impressions of childhood, the grasp of language, and the impact of culture give him a vehicle for expressing his hidden self. The Supreme Word finds words.

So it is in meditation. The practitioner starts in silence, where the mystery remains as yet unknown to mind or heart. At first only the depths of the human spirit know the depths of the divine indwelling Spirit and so the meditator remains quiet and still. Gradually the experiences of meditation and the movements of the Spirit begin to reveal the quality of spirit.

Although the practitioner receives the teachings of the master and recites the mantra, it is only when Spirit reveals to spirit, only when there is realization, that the meditator at last comes to understand the true nature within and the gift that has been given.

For the practitioner, weakness of character, personal and inherited sins obscure the light, but in the case of the young Jesus, his clarity of character and the simplicity of Mary's influence make him realize his true nature all the more quickly so that at the age of twelve he declares himself.

As the Gospel of Luke recounts, he leaves his parents. Much to the anguish of Mary and Joseph he cannot be found. What if he has been kidnapped or killed or injured or abused? How could he do this to them? At last they find him in the Temple. He then declares, with all the candour of youth, that the One his ancestors worshipped is really 'My Father', for he has come to know his inner nature, his essential relationship. He is of God and for God, uniquely.

The remainder of his life, the next twenty-one years, are simply the living out of this realization.

So too the practitioner, who comes to the calm centre, the still point where there is no further questioning, acquires the central experience that fills heart and life. The meditator comes to personal truth, the essential word, the inner core that informs all other truths.

4. The man

He rises up out of the waters and hears the Voice from heaven, 'You are my Son, the Beloved'. What waves of joy and triumph must thrill through him! In the Temple some twenty years earlier he had spoken of his Father. Now the God of Israel addresses him: 'You are my son'. He is claimed and acclaimed. There is no reaction among the bystanders. Jesus alone is addressed and he alone hears. Yet the Voice fills the whole world.

The meditator can continue to meditate only if, equivalently but perhaps more obscurely, the Voice has rung in him or her, declaring who they are and choosing them. Meditation is a voyage of discovery not only of God but also of oneself. Indeed the two discoveries are one, for the knowledge of God and the realization of the self coincide. What then does the meditator acknowledge about his or her own self? Who are they to themselves? What word defines them and fills them with joy and triumph?

Jesus had entered into the waters of the Jordan and tasted the waters of death. And his rising from the muddy stream prefigures his resurrection. He already knows, in a sense, both death and life. Because he accepts to be sacrificed, he is shown to be Son of God, Lord of both the living and the dead. He stands triumphant on the bank of the river, empowered and authorized.

In the quiet of meditation, when all other agendas are abandoned, the truest nature is revealed, purpose and mission are understood. Self-knowledge and the knowledge of one's destiny coincide. The stillness of meditation communicates energy and an outpouring of activity.

The Spirit descends on Jesus like the dove that came to Noah's ark bearing the olive branch of peace and consecration.

What sense of peace comes upon the practitioner, what sense of divine acceptance and self-acceptance? The Spirit descends as the proof of divine favour. The practitioner is beloved.

Jesus comes to knowledge, but the fullness of knowledge is given only when he enters the totality of death and is raised to the highest heaven. The fullness of knowledge is available only beyond this world.

Similarly the meditator comes to a certain level of knowledge while realizing at the same time that its fullness coincides with the resurrection of the dead, on the last day.

LENT

There are many areas of need, many wounds, not only in the body but also in the memory and in the heart and in the spirit. All need to be healed for all are wounded.

Christian meditation provides the surest means of healing at the ultimate level for it worships a Christ who, alone among all the great spiritual leaders on the earth, was so cruelly put to death. 'Crucified yet risen' (Mark 16:6), he is able to sympathize with all who live in the limitations of weakness (Hebrew 5:1-2) and his sympathy is not a powerless emotion.

1. The return to the origins — ash

Yahweh God fashioned the man of dust from the soil. Then he
breathed into his nostrils a breath of life. (Genesis 2:7)

Meditation is an invitation to abandon anxiety and to return to the desert from which all life springs. It involves an inner act of trust, the belief, indeed the knowledge, that despite all appearances the Source of the universe is essentially good and that human destiny is essentially fair. It involves a cessation of desire, even of the desire for good health. It involves accepting to lose all and to place hope in the One who formed humankind, somehow, from the clay of earth.

Thus the first and primary step in the process of healing is to trust in the Origin, in oneself and in the future, which trust is the work of the Spirit, for 'God breathed into his nostrils a breath of life'; or again, 'the first man, being from the earth, was earthly; the last Adam has become a life-giving spirit' (1 Corinthians 15:45, 47).

It is not a return to the past, for the past can never be regained. It is a return to the origins, with the knowledge that the Beginning and the End will bring about a state so full that all the sorrows of the past are forgotten.

This is not passivity, but a renewal of energy, for the return to the Origin gives authority, as when Adam stood on the earth and was master of all he saw. We are in charge of our own healing, not as though we are separate from our Origin but because we have returned to it. As the Preface for Sundays III states: 'Man [sic] refused your friendship but man himself was to restore it through Jesus Christ our Lord'.

The practitioner begins by placing ash on the body to acknowledge that all is made of dust and will return to dust. This smearing with ash shows that the practitioner already transcends ash, like the phoenix rising. With the smearing of the ash, either done literally or more importantly done with unreserved intention, the heart achieves the quiet, by which alone body, mind and spirit are healed.

The essential method is knowing that all are destined to life, not death and that the present frailty is itself frail and only a passing thing.

2. The healing Spirit — incense

And Yahweh God breathed into his nostrils a breath of life, and thus the man became a living being. (Genesis 2:7)

The problem of evil has always troubled the human spirit. Is there a malevolent force at work, a dark god battling the God of Light? Is evil mere chance, a throw of the dice? Is it due to some personal or ancestral sin (John 9:2) or due to the sin of Adam? Am I guilty as well as sick? Is there a solution or is despair the only real response?

The loss of everything, of health and possessions, of relationships and life, means entering the fog of desolation. The horror of sin overwhelms. It is impossible to explain evil, for evil does not make sense and would not be evil if it could be understood. Evil cannot be justified but it can be turned to good. Just as Jesus lay in the cold of death and was raised by the Father's glory (Romans 8.11), so, even when all seems reduced to dust, a Breath stirs that could hardly be perceived before.

The Spirit is a healing Breath, and the cloud of incense with its captivating perfume well symbolizes this Holy Spirit. The Spirit is the Breath of Life, the unfailing fount welling up from the deep aquifers of being. This is the Breath humanity wishes for, the Spirit in the spirit, Spirit perceptible at first only to spirit. Brought to darkness, nothing is seen, nothing known, but we are present to the Presence, the healing, comforting Presence.

The inspiring Spirit moves powerfully and radiates out from the human spirit into the mind and into the emotions and into the body, bringing healing, perhaps not immediately, perhaps not before our bodies crumble into dust, but eventually, when all time is done. In the deepest recesses of the human spirit an energy is felt and a joy, even while the body is ill at ease. An empowering faith is felt which moves mountains and which brings the dead to life and produces the new creation. This Spirit saves.

When all this happens, when evil and even sin have been turned to advantage, when the heights and the depths have been explored, then all suffering will be forgotten as a mother forgets the labour of childbirth.

(John16:21) We will at last understand the relationship of good and evil and will call out with the cherubim, 'Holy, Holy, Holy is the Lord of hosts', for he has shown himself to be utterly faithful even when all seems absurd and terrible.

3. Healing the will — water

However, a flood was rising from the earth and watering all
the surface of the soil ... A river flowed from Eden to water the
garden and from there it divided to make four streams.
(Genesis 2:6, 10)

The hands are plunged deep into the water to feel its cooling touch. This world of anxiety and injustice is abandoned. Indecision and regrettable acts are rejected. Restrictions and burdens are left behind as we plunge into the depths, without thought, without desire, without any precondition, led to the Spirit by the Spirit.

Water cleanses. There in the water a rebirth occurs. Life's purpose is rediscovered, the essential orientation and new mind free of guilt or blame.

The Spirit is given as a gift. The Spirit freely chooses to make free. The Spirit freely makes us freely choose to be free. No one is forced to be free. It is the moment of grace.

The Spirit is not some foreign substance introduced from outside. The wish to place the hands in the cleansing stream is due to the Sprit who rises and waters the earth before even the first human being is formed.

The water rises before the figure of clay is shaped on the earth. Humans exist in God before existing as creatures. The Spirit hovers over the deep before ever the light was made (Genesis 1:1-2). Human destiny is intended before time begins. The true self is the future self and the future self is the transfigured body.

The meditator sits quietly. Then, perhaps, the meditator may feel inspired to place both hands deep in the water, to feel its refreshing touch, to submerge in the Spirit who is welling within and to assent to the Spirit transmuting the will, inspiring the practitioner to choose the true self. Sitting quietly, the practitioner merges into the healing Spirit and finds the will transformed. The whole person is immersed in the refreshing Spirit, who fills the universe.

4. Healing the memory — words

'It is not good that the man should be alone. I will make him a helpmate.' So from the soil Yahweh God fashioned all the wild beasts ... The man gave names to all the cattle, all the birds of heaven and all the wild beasts ...' (Genesis 2:18-20)

Each person carries scars in the heart where words have cut deep: words said in jest or malice, truths too hard to bear, lies, false teaching, words of abuse. Words hurt especially when they come from those who are dear. There are also wounds caused by words that were not said, the dreadful silences where no one said 'Well done', or 'I love you'. The wounds go deep into the flesh and dwell there; they go into the memory and infect every choice.

What is true of words is also true of events because words are deeds and deeds are words.

The words and events that distort family and social history also affect the individual who takes descent from them. The lives of ancestors are in a sense the past lives of their descendents who spring from them and inherit their stories as well as their genes. Bad memories can be inherited and must be healed. The negative mental patterning must be cleared.

The past cannot be undone but it can be redeemed and turned to good, for wounds open the heart to hear more powerful words. Memory is healed by a stronger memory. The impact of the wounding words must be softened and even negated — which can happen if the Spirit gives the words of Jesus full force in our memory so that the words of Jesus are preferred. The meditator thus goes back before these events to a higher power and an earlier intention.

The meditator first faces the bad memory and allows it to rise up in all its destructive power. Then the words of Jesus are recalled. He says, 'I have loved you with an everlasting love' (Hosea 2:21), and 'See, I put my words in your mouth ...' (Jeremiah :.9), and 'Fear not' (John 6:20), and 'Behold I make all things new' (Revelations 21:5). Jesus wishes the practitioner to attain the true self, that self whom others, with the practitioner's unwitting connivance, have suppressed. This is possible only by the Holy Spirit, 'who teaches us everything and reminds us of all that Jesus has said to us' (John 14:26).

Each bad memory is reviewed and replaced with the words of the one Saviour to whom full authority is given, both by the practitioner and by heaven itself.

5. Healing the emotions — oil of chrism

Yahweh God said: 'It is not good that the man should be alone. I will make him a helpmate'. (Genesis 2:18)

In themselves, emotions are not a good guide. There can be fear where there is nothing to fear. There can be feasting while Rome burns. Highs and lows can jostle each other for no reason. Fear, guilt, anxiety and resentments can inhibit and overwhelm. Who does not long for a steady joy, a sense of vigour and well-being?

Where does the emotion come from? Is the feeling of resentment due to real injury or to wounded pride? Is the hurt deep or superficial? Is the wound beyond healing or is it the opportunity for a new direction in life? Are the fears real or based on attitudes which have been adopted? Is depression because of repressed anger or to the absence of relationship? Do the tensions come from the pace of modern life or to unresolved issues in the home?

Debilitating emotions can come from a breakdown of relationships. 'It is not good that the man should be alone.' Everyone needs a companion to give stability and joy. 'I shall make him a helpmate.' Has the art of friendship been lost? Have the events of life or poor socializing skills alienated all friends?

The meditator observes the emotions, whether of joy or sadness. Tranquillity comes from looking on pain or pleasure equally. Rejecting an emotion will only make it fester. Seeking an emotion that does not arise spontaneously is to play charades. Facing grief means transcending it and to savour joy is to make it go deep.

The meditator sits quietly and faces an emotion and then touches the oil of chrism and places it on the forehead. It is the soothing balm, the symbol of the Spirit giving love and peace, self-control (Galations 5:22). The consolation of the Spirit can restore some balance, for the Spirit is oil poured on troubled waters. Faced with human emotion in all its complexity the emotion of the Spirit is inserted into the equation. It is the work of faith that heals all things.

6. Healing the body

But no helpmate suitable for the man was found for him.

68

So Yahweh God made the man fall into a deep sleep. And while
he slept, he took one of his ribs and enclosed it in flesh. Yahweh
God built the rib he had taken from the man into a woman
(Genesis 2:20-22)

The image of Adam and Eve in the garden in the full freshness of youth is entrancing but liable to misinterpretation. It teaches the truth that the human condition is essentially good and destined to happiness, but it can be misleading if sickness and death have to be explained as punishment.

It is true nevertheless that a disturbance of the emotions can affect a person bodily. A distorted will is particularly injurious because the human being is body, mind, and spirit all together, as a harmonious whole.

The spiritual psychosomatic complex can only be healed by spirit, mind and matter. All the forms of preventive and curative medicine are to be used, good diet, healthy life-style, etc. But meditation goes further since it balances all the faculties and brings them into coherence with the mind of God, so that the vitality of God flows into the practitioner. By resting in the Silence, the stress and turmoil of life ceases and the exhausted spirit is revitalized.

Adam who has named the creatures and shown himself their master has failed to find what satisfies him. He therefore falls into a deep sleep and there, surprisingly, the solution is found. In a way he does not know, the companion is formed who will bring creation to its perfection.

By allowing the body to adopt a position of alert restfulness, all the faculties are brought into balance. Meditation is an attitude of expectancy without presuming the outcome, of hope without desire for anything the limited mind might crave. Meditation does not mean denying age or death but allowing these their place along with youth and success. Disability and pain are faced and seen for what they are. They do not define the human being, for they can be observed and then transcended. Meditation involves rising beyond life and death and reaching the One who makes all fall into the deep sleep of death and brings the Spirit who unlocks the hidden springs of life and regenerates from within.

7. Healing relationships

The man exclaimed: 'This at last is bone from my bones and flesh from my flesh! ... 'This is why a man ... joins himself to his wife, and they become one body. (Genesis 2:23)

The greatest joys and the most intense pain are found in relationships, yet these are least under control of the person. Everyone has experienced wounds in their relationships, whether with parents or children or spouse or colleagues. Most people want to love but do not know how to love or find no one to love. Yet all are made for love and cannot be themselves apart from others. How to heal the wounded heart or find a companion?

The meditator begins by observing and admitting a faulty relationship, without apportioning blame or raking over past hurts. It is a question of seeing what is, and if there must be anger it is at the wastefulness and pity. Such an approach is possible only if the Spirit moves. Meditation gives space for the Spirit to seep into the mind and eventually to become strong. The meditator is gradually healed of the hurt and is no longer afraid or resentful or negative and has the strength to look beyond.

As the impulse of the Spirit becomes strong, the meditator is able to project that Spirit of kindness and forgiveness, the Spirit of freedom and fidelity, the Spirit of love that does not demand to be requited, a fire which warms and does not burn.

However, this attitude — it must be said — will only cause more pain since it is so demanding: it is a share in the passion. It seems easier to repay hurt with hurt, but revenge only compounds the problem. To love the unloving requires a divine power.

By projecting the fire of the Spirit the opponent may be won over. This is the sweetest victory: freely to bring a person to choose freely to mend a broken relationship. Indeed the lesson learnt with such great difficulty makes the original breakdown of relationships worthwhile — a blessed fault.

Even if the love remains unrequited the meditator has come to that perfect compassion, which makes its sun to shine on just and unjust alike (Matthew 5:45).

The Sacred Triduum

1. Exhalation

'Blessed are the poor in spirit, the kingdom of heaven is theirs.'
(Matthew 5:3)

Blessed are the truly poor, for they attach no essential importance to wealth or status or health or anything that can be possessed. They rely only on what transcends all passing things and are in stark contrast with a society where the rich and famous, the successful and the beautiful, attract attention.

Jesus perfectly illustrates his teaching on the day of his passion when he is stripped of clothing and dignity. He is nailed to a cross and rendered powerless. No justice is granted to him and even God seems to abandon him as he surrenders in death. He is poor in every way.

The four gospels differ in their presentation of Jesus' last moments. The first two emphasize his sense of abandonment when he cries out, 'My God, my God, why have you abandoned me?' (Matthew 27.47; Mark 15.34) Luke and especially John present the paradox of Jesus' ignominy and triumph. Jesus, naked and crucified, proclaims victoriously, 'It is accomplished' (John 19:30).

Jesus endures complete poverty but knows that kingdom of heaven is his. All authority in heaven and earth is given to him; all ages and powers are placed in his hands. He takes all creation and all humanity to himself so that he holds all things together in unity in his own being. He is all and all is his.

Expiration is an anticipation of the last breath, the total poverty of death, and is indeed an experience of Calvary.

The first word of the Beatitudes is the word 'blessed'. God dwells in perfect bliss, indeed is perfect bliss, unattached, transcending the goods of the world, which are the limited expressions of God's being. It is the bliss of freedom, and knowledge and blessing. It is the happiness of perfect light without any shadow or illusion; of love without hesitation or fear; of unlimited being and perfect peace. It is the bliss, which blesses.

After the breath has been emitted there is a pause before the lungs automatically begin to fill again. This is a moment of peace and tranquility. The focus is applied there, in that moment of peace when all the bother of life comes to its point of rest. It is symbolic of the immense calm of God. It is a time of transcendence, a moment of truth and already a taste of paradise.

2. Inhalation and exhalation

'Blessed are those who mourn, they shall be comforted.'
(Matthew 5:5)

'Those who mourn' are not callous or insensitive, for they feel the loss and anguish of others as if they were their own. They do not turn away but identify with those in trouble. They do so not out of guilt but out of compassion, and they enter into the condition of others so as to stand with them.

Jesus himself is one who mourns since, as the Creed states, 'for us and for our salvation he came down from heaven and became man'. Out of compassion he enters into the limitations of human existence. He is sent from above to enter into the sin of the world. He mourns with the lost and shares their sense of abandonment. Indeed he goes further into distress, for only the one who is above all can be brought lower than all.

The meditator focuses firstly on the inhalation, and breathes in all the pain of the world, all its mess, all that is repulsive and unpalatable. The inhalation is an identification with the pain of others and may be accompanied by a visualization of a situation. Thus there is a real identification with the situation of others.

Those who mourn, the text goes on, 'shall be comforted' It is a promise, for the act of compassion leads to a higher plane. Conversely, dwelling at the higher level, indeed the supreme level of heaven itself, leads to further compassion. A divine energy and peace arise within and spread out to others. Compassion empowers.

Jesus is comforted on the day of the resurrection when he is raised from the dead by the Father's glory, namely by the Spirit, the Comforter. Into him streams happiness of every sort and from him stream blessings of every type.

Accordingly, the meditator, after having inhaled the sorrows of the world, breathes out happiness upon all.

3. Inhalation

'Blessed are the pure in heart; they shall see God.'
(Matthew 5:8)

The pure in heart are without duplicity or secret agendas, without divided loyalties or hostility, but consistent and integrated.

'They shall see God', not just with their spirits and minds but with their eyes as well. 'And in my flesh I shall see God' (Job 19:27). God will be seen in every aspect of their lives. Tears as well as joys, strengths and even sins will reveal God, for God is greater than human weakness. A sense of thanks will swell from the heart and reveal itself in praise: thanks for the shadow as well as for the radiance.

The in-drawing of breath has many meanings: the gasp of delight, the sigh of relief, the welcome inhalation of freshness after squalour. Inhalation is first experienced at birth and is the foretaste of immortal life. It is felt as an intoxication of delight and forecasts the resurrection from the dead. The vast expanse of air surrounding the planet is drawn into the nostrils and tells of the vast surrounding Spirit.

Knowing this, the meditator focuses, without reflection, simply on the inhalation and allows it to work its enlivening effect, which leads eventually to the knowledge of the divine Giver.

HOLY SATURDAY

He emptied himself ... He was humbler yet, even to accepting death, death on a cross. But God raised him high ...
(Philippians 2:7-9)

1. The stillness of the tomb

One of the most beautiful images is surely the face on the Shroud of Turin that purports to show Jesus in death. The face is serene, both radiant and inward. In fact it does not seem to show a corpse but someone who is aware of every depth and height; majestic, the face of truth.

The tomb of Jesus is the sacred place, the point of transition between death and life, between earth and heaven, time and eternity, the place of the resurrection which is not an event like any other but the abandonment of any particular time and place, indeed the filling of every time and place.

Meditation is a joining with Christ in the stillness of the tomb.

The frantic activity of the day is put aside and the practitioner first becomes still because the balance between outward and inward, upward and downward, has been perfectly achieved. Neither attitude is adopted too much, each in its own way is accepted. This is done from the purest of motives. Meditation is the place of obedience designated by the divine will and chosen wholeheartedly by the meditator.

In response to this universal attentiveness, the divine Heart suddenly appears, for it will not resist the attentive heart. Heart speaks to heart in the stillness of the one Heart. The divine mind and the meditator's mind coincide.

Thus the meditation room becomes the sacred precinct where the temple of the body has been erected. The meditator's postures, the simply being here, is a blessing to all. The turning away from fractious activity coincides with the most unified and powerful effectiveness.

2. The withdrawal of the senses

The stone is rolled across the tomb and sealed shut. The eyes of Jesus that can see no more have nothing to see. The withdrawal of the senses is complete. Although Jesus will appear in the room and again taste fish (Luke 24:43), that is only a sign. Essentially Jesus has withdrawn from this world.

From the start Jesus intended not only to become flesh (John 1:14) but also to become perfect flesh in perfect flesh. This is the glory that he desired from the beginning and the reason why he took on the horror of the cross. He does not shield his eyes for knows he has the strength of his divinity to contemplate the extremes.

So too the meditator withdraws from all sensation so that the senses might be brought to their highest state. This act of withdrawing does not eliminate the senses but empowers them. They are sharpened and sensitized.

It is possible to withdraw only if there is a depth within. It is the vertigo of the abyss. This withdrawal of the senses puts the meditator in touch with the power of that essential heart so that the meditator is transformed and made able to see things unimagined. Like Christ, the meditator looks upon creation and refashions it. Whether the eyes are open or closed the same reality is seen, for the meditator transforms all into a reflection of the light within.

Even though Exodus states that 'no one can see God and live' (33:20), the risen person will with immortal eyes look upon the eternal God. 'From my flesh I shall see God' (Job 19:26). Transfigured in the light of Tabor, the risen person is able to see the Divine Light. 'We shall see God as he really is' (I John 3:2).

The emptying has led to fullness.

3. From ignorance to knowledge

When things fall apart, when hopes are dashed and the body shows its fragility, when relationships turn sour and grief shakes the foundations of life, not only do physical and emotional pain attack the senses but the mind and the heart become clouded as well. Nothing has meaning and the sense of God disappears. It is the spiritual breakdown. The problem of evil has always been the most telling reason for rejecting any idea of God.

So too Jesus cries out, 'Why have you deserted me?' (Matthew 27:47), and there is no answer to his question. Ignorance enters his soul.

But the collapse lays bare a deeper knowledge. The thought constructs and all the barriers are dismantled. All the controlling labels fall off, limitations cease, and another awareness arises, which is consciousness without thought. Theology gives way to mysticism, discursive meditation gives way to contemplation, thought surrenders to presence in the cloud of unknowing. It is a process of discovery. There is an awareness of grace and truth, which may be suggested by poetry and expressed in symbols, but never contained. There is no longer the haze of question and answer; nothing obstructs pure Presence, which is peaceful, splendid, intimate and available in every direction and in every time.

So Jesus, who has entered the darkness of tomb and soul, is fully present to his God. He is beyond time and space and any limitation and, therefore, his bones can be in no one place and his heart cannot be confined. Through his ignorance he has come to the only knowledge which truly counts, and amazed at the drama of the passion he ascends to heaven crying out 'Holy, Holy, Holy'.

The meditator who, like Jesus, goes through the process of moving through ignorance to knowledge is not hampered by thoughts and ideas or ambitions. God is present to the practitioner and the practitioner is present to God. From the whole person of the meditator blessings stream. The meditator is fully present to all and all is present to the meditator. It is the victory. It is the recreation of Easter Sunday morning.

4. From 'no' to 'yes'

'No', says the child as it tries to define itself and come to a sense of individuality. 'Yes', says the consumerist society to itself and 'no' to others who might be a threat. The quality of 'yes' and 'no' define the character of a person and their spiritual depth. The saint says 'yes' to all that affirms and 'no' to all that negates.

Jesus lies in the tomb because they had said 'no' to him and rejected the One who sent him. But Jesus had said 'yes' to humanity when he chose to become flesh, 'yes' to the excluded and the despised as he ate with them, and 'yes' to his One who sent him when he accepted the bitter cup of the passion.

Jesus is the great 'Amen' (Revelations 3:14), not 'yes' and 'no' but simply 'yes' (2 Corinthians 1:20). It is not the 'yes' of the weak-willed or indiscriminate but the 'yes' which disarms. To those who labour under all the resentment and uncontrolled desire: in their inmost ear Jesus whispers 'yes' for their redemption. To rejection he replies with universal acceptance and unconditional love.

Meditation is a profound affirmation. The depths of the Spirit remain closed if there are unresolved issues or points of misunderstanding. Peace is both the prelude to meditation and constitutes its purpose: peace with oneself, with one's neighbour and with the Ultimate, a peace that is peace-making. Peace is utter self-consistence. The meditator who comes to peace becomes peace and is identified with the One who is Peace. There is one Peace. Meditation cannot take place in fear or in resentment, in guilt or in denial. Meditation is at heart a 'yes'.

The meditator sits, refusing nothing, blocking nothing, rejecting nothing and open to all, available to all, accepting all, saying 'yes' to the heart of all.

5. From desolation to consolation

As he realizes the horror of what lies ahead and how bitter is the cup he must drink, Jesus feels his heart fail within him, and he becomes 'sorrowful to the point of death' (Mark 14:34). His disciples abandon him and his people turn against him. Even if an angel comes as the text says (Luke 22:43) his agony is only all the greater, for the Holy Spirit is withdrawing from him. He is distressed and increasingly broken, for the Spirit is emptying from his spirit.

Likewise in meditation, the time comes when all consolation goes, leaving dryness and desolation. There is no pleasure, no apparent fruitfulness, and no motivation. Yet the meditator cannot abandon meditation but is driven to it, as Jesus was driven into the desert and driven to the cross.

The memory of past consolations and above all the persistent if hidden inspiration of the Spirit do not let the meditator go. The practitioner is both inspired to meditate and uninspired in his meditation. It is the stripping down to the essential, the absorption, and a retreat from the outer levels to the inner core. The Spirit has left the emotions and the mind and even the will and speaks only to the spirit, the divine Depth speaking to the human depth. 'Deep calling unto deep' (Psalm 42:7). It is the driest desert.

Yet this is the most important moment. The emptying is the filling. It is the re-creation of the whole person on the basis of the Spirit alone. The meditator is re-created, re-formed as an entirely spiritual person, in every domain. Through having dried up without the gentle rain of the Spirit, the practitioner now regenerates as completely inspired. As fire must race through the bush if the seeds are to break open and germinate, so must the fire of the Spirit consume everything that does not belong to the Spirit, so that the fruits of the Spirit may become apparent. The meditator's body is spiritual, the meditatir's mind is inspired, the meditator's spirit is Spirit.

Thus the moment of desolation coincides with the moment of consolation. The complete abandonment of all else is pleasing to the Spirit. The pouring out of the life blood is irresistible to the Spirit who then comes in all fullness, Spirit to spirit, 'deep calling to deep in the roar of the mighty flood' (Psalm 42:7) of the blood poured out, to give blessing and power.

The Spirit now acts in all fullness, raising Jesus from the dead and transforming him in every respect so that he is totally inspired, totally spiritual (1 Corinthians 15:45). His body and every aspect can no longer remain lifeless and located in time and place but are fully inspired, fully free and omnipresent beyond ordinary observation.

6. From death to life

Jesus is dead. The God-man is no more. He is brought to nothing.

In one sense the incarnation is complete: the Word became mortal flesh and that vulnerability has now been shown in its totality. In another sense the incarnation has failed since Jesus is no longer human. The incarnation is complete when it has ceased.

The God-man has been brought to nothing and God has been brought to nothing, so it seems. Jesus has been silenced and eliminated so that God too has been silenced and made ineffectual. With the death of the God-man his God has been removed from all consideration. It is the 'death of God', the emptying of heaven itself, so it seems, leaving only idols in the minds of Jesus' opponents.

The meditator sits still and silent, inactive and seemingly irrelevant. The meditation seems useless and ineffectual. But the meditator is also a puzzle, a challenge, even someone to be feared. What is going on? What secret experiences are occurring? How check their value? External expression can be controlled but the inner life is free. Here is something out of control: if it is false it cannot be detected; if it is truly the work of God it upsets all the constructs. The meditator is both asleep and fully awake, as though dead yet fully alive.

Jesus, as he lies emptied of life and awaits the resurrection, is the prototype of the meditator. His is a strategic withdrawal. He has allowed the worst to happen and will show that it is powerless. The seeming victory of his opponents is mere folly. He will leave the tomb and fill the universe, reaching heaven itself.

7. Atheism — God is all in all

The time comes to enter completely into the cloud. All ideas go, nothing makes sense. Even the teachings of the faith do not satisfy. All ideas of

God, even the sense of commitment go. There are no sensations of joy in the Spirit. There is no will and no wish. Yet this is not a disturbing time; there is peacefulness about entering into complete ignorance and absence of desire.

Jesus lies dead in the tomb; the stone is rolled over the entrance and the disciples leave. There is nothing; there is everything. '*Nada, todo*', says John of the Cross. 'Nothing, everything.'

The meditator comes to that point where there is nothing. It is a daring, bold moment. It is a turning away from all that has been received and an entry into the immediate, without preconception or ambition of any sort. It is an indifference to whether God exists or not. There is no depending, no yearning. It is a sort of atheism. It is openness to whatever may be the case since there is nothing that can obstruct. It is a fearless facing of the truth no matter how unpalatable. It is a total frankness.

This attitude is a liberation from the baggage of other people's ideas and experiences. Social and ecclesial pressures have been set aside.

It is then that the presence of God appears in all truth. Any idea of God is less than God. Any desire for God denotes the absence of God. There are now no ideas but only the immediacy of divine knowledge. There is no desire or seeking, for all is present. The Presence eliminates all ideas, for they are no longer relevant. The Presence makes all desire unnecessary, for what more could be desired? There is no separation, for presence involves identity. The meditator is present to the Presence in an eternal present. There is only Presence.

This occurs at the deepest level, in the very fountainhead of one's being, and permeates the whole person, totally transforming and refashioning every element and faculty, so that everything is consumed in the fire of the Presence. Every element of body, mind, and spirit is taken into the Presence and transformed into Presence. The meditator is simply present to the Presence, one Presence.

Therefore the tomb is empty and Jesus is the sacrament of the divine Presence, throughout heaven and earth. There is only Presence. God is all in all.

EASTERTIDE

1. Renewing relationships

... the doors were closed in the room where the disciples
were, out of fear ... Jesus came and stood among them.
(John. 20:19)

A wounded relationship is least easily healed for it involves another's
freedom over which there is no control. The doors seem firmly shut and
cannot be opened, for fear inhabits the trauma.

The meditator first acknowledges the trauma, facing the facts in all
their pitiableness and rising above aversion and desire, acquiring equanimity towards the passing nature of both beauty and horror.

This equanimity involves transcending the ego and discovering the
real self, for the ego is a fictitious self, a self-image fabricated out of
opinions and limited conditions. Nevertheless, abandoning the ego is
difficult, for it involves a sort of death.

'Jesus stood among them.' In the stillness of meditation the true self
appears. The wounding has stripped away illusions and cravings.
Jesus stands there and likewise the meditator is simply there. Nothing can
close Jesus out and nothing can finally shut the meditator off from their
real self, and so life begins in another dimension. This is possible because

Jesus, in some moment of grace, has been able to penetrate the fears. The practitioner believes in him and so can believe in themselves. The meditator knows Jesus and so realizes an identity of nature with him.

Those who have hurt and betrayed also live behind closed doors but the meditator penetrates spiritually into their presence. Like Jesus, the practitioner has no wish or even thought of taking revenge on them. Having abandoned the ego the practitioner is better aware of them. Having discovered the true self, the practitioner knows of their true self so that the meditator is more understanding and compassionate, more sensitive to their pain and fears. All this involves an unconditional and infinite love that the antagonist can hardly resist, for the freedom of unconditional love unbinds those who have done harm. In their regard the meditator has become Christ risen.

The heart swells with thanks that all this has happened. It is the moment of redemption.

2. Renewing the body

He showed them his hands and his side. The disciples were filled with joy when they saw the Lord. (John 20:20)

The human body is frail even though 'it is marvellously made' (Psalm 139:14) The vulnerable flesh is eventually mortally wounded and good health only delays the fateful day when the cry is heard, 'Who shall free us from this body of death?' (Romans 7:24).

Although history has seen many great spiritual leaders, only one, the Crucified, has known the full range of joy and pain, glory and humiliation. He knows good and evil as none other can know and in the breadth of this knowledge knows the infinite God. He stands without shame before the world as 'Lord of the dead and the living'. (Romans 14:9)

The meditator openly contemplates human frailty. 'He showed them his hands and his side.' The meditator enters the calm of truth, for the experience of good and evil reveals the Transcendent God, taking us beyond this pleasant world to the hidden dimension from which all things come.

Blessings stream from the wounds, although they are scandalous and distressing. 'The disciples were filled with joy when they saw the Lord' because they know that he had been raised. The Spirit streams out from the wounds as did the blood and water when the side was pierced. This is the paradox, which is incomprehensible since it is of the very nature of the inexplicable God. The cross is planted in heaven itself.

Power streams out from the wounds of the innocent. Of course, health is to be sought where health can be found, but the inevitable decay becomes a blessing because God is holy. Eternity does not remove the wounds but transfigures them. The wounds of the Just One are glorious and so are those of the innocent.

The meditator focuses on the wound, whatever it may be, communicating the Word, the mantra; and imparts the Spirit, the breath, making the injury radiant with light. The whole of creation proceeds from the Word. Likewise, from the essential word that constitutes the practitioner's very being the whole person is made new. In meditation the practitioner becomes aware of what this word is and becomes aware of what the future shall be. The mantra is the seed, which develops into the great tree of eternity. In the power of this knowledge the human being is remade.

The true healing of body consists not in becoming young again but in making the body victorious over death. The healing is complete once thanks are given for the wound, while full thanks are possible only at the resurrection of the dead.

3. Renewing the emotions

*Jesus came and stood among them. He said to them, 'Peace
be with you' ... The disciples were filled with joy ...'*
(John 20:20)

Jesus stands among them and offers the greeting of peace because he is
peace. He stands at the centre of the vortex; he has gone beyond good
and evil and rests in his own self.

The meditator adopts a position of rest, seated at ease but not too
easy, alert but not tense. The emotions are like a maelstrom in their
circling restlessness, but the meditator remains tranquil at their centre.
Something beyond human control, some grace, leads the practitioner to
the quiet heart where the fluctuating mind is irrelevant. Like the arms of
the beam balance, which cease to oscillate and rest perfectly still, the
meditator ceases to be exaggeratedly extrovert or introvert, outward or
inward but is all these in equal measure. At the first stage of meditation
the practitioner faces the tumult of the emotions but ceases to be dis-
turbed by them. The unquiet heart comes to its rest.

Then comes a surge of energy. On reaching the place where the
heart finds its treasure, there is a burst of happiness. 'The disciples were
filled with joy when they saw the Lord.' The meditator is both at peace
and totally involved in all the emotions that spring from him. They are
accepted and unambiguously experienced, intense and full, pure and
whole hearted. By going beyond emotion, the meditator enters into all
the emotions. The practitioner possesses them but is not possessed by
them; enjoys them but does not depend on them.

The practitioner remains tranquil while being fully involved in the
rough and tumble of daily life. Joy and happiness surge from within and
do not depend on external circumstances.

This peace cannot be contained, for peace has an innate energy. Only the truly restful person can be fully active where the restless person is distracted and divided. Perfect rest and highest activity imply each other. Peace makes peace and joy enjoys, so that vitality eddies out to transform all. The meditator too stands at the centre and says, 'Peace be with you', and the world is filled with joy.

4. Renewing the memory

He said to them again, 'Peace be with you. As the Father sent me, so I am sending you'. (John 20:21)

Memory is a powerful tool, for good and ill. Past experiences are preserved there and bear their fruit; good memories bear sweet fruit, bad memories rotten fruit.

Meditation can heal the memory because it takes us beyond memory. By going upstream to the pristine source, before the muddying of the waters, we can drink deeply and attain what was to come, for the Christian meditator connects with the Word 'through whom all things were made' (John 1:2). From the Word, and even from the Word-made-flesh, all times and all memories proceed.

'As the Father sent me.' The incarnate Word is sent to the world in all its weakness, a beam of light in the murkiness of the world that he at once reveals and dispels. In turn he sends the meditator: 'So I am sending you'. Where to? The meditator is sent in the first instance to their own memory and to those who produced those past experiences, good or bad. Further, the meditator is sent not just to the memory of things past but also to the anticipation of things future. Hope and fear, trauma and pleasure: to all of these the meditator is sent, and not just to personal memories but also to the sorrows of others, indeed to what haunts whole nations. By regaining that original clarity of vision, the meditator faces and heals the memories.

The meditator understands that the events of history can be healed and empowered. Their knowledge, that from the beginning humanity is destined for something greater and is heir to things beyond imagining, will like the birth of a child, blot out the memory of the pain.

More than that! The trauma opens the horizons. Greater powers are called into play and made available. There is a movement from weakness to strength. Far from remaining frozen by the bad experience the meditator turns it into an advantage.

When this happens, a song of thanksgiving springs up and the bad experience is blessed for having swept through the forest like a fire, cracking open the waiting seed.

5. From sin to love

... he breathed on them and said: 'Receive the Holy Spirit. For those whose sins you forgive they are forgiven; for those who sins you retain they are retained'. (John 20:22-23)

Sin is in the will and, likewise, love is in the will, so that every sin is a form of hate. While the hateful act may give some relief, in the long run it is self-destructive. The teaching, 'eye for eye, tooth for tooth' (Exodus 21:24) is already a limitation on hate but is not yet perfect love which commands, 'love your enemies and to do good to those who hate you' (Luke 6:27).

Jesus breathes on the disciples and on the whole church.

The meditator imagines the breath of the Lord reaching right into the lungs. This breath is symbolic of the Holy Spirit and is indeed the communication of the Spirit so that the practitioner has a sense of unstinted life moving within, which is known by faith, for faith is the immense sensitivity that reaches to the farthest distance.

The meditator then focuses on the sin of the world neither denying the evil nor seeking revenge but replacing the curse with a blessing. The wrong is not approved but shown to be insignificant compared to the greater power of the Spirit. The Breath that has been received, the Holy Spirit, is breathed out upon those who are marked by hate and so replaces the seeds of death in them with the source of life. This act does not mask the sin but reaches into the heart of the 'enemy', there to sow the seeds of kindness. It requires immense courage and strength of character, peacefulness of heart and compassion. It takes the practitioner out of time and into the mind of God.

APPENDIX

Visualization

1. The face of Jesus

The Word was made flesh,
he lived amongst us and we saw his glory,
the glory that was his as the only Son of the Father,
full of grace and truth. (John 1.14)

Many descriptions of Jesus are given in the gospels: shepherd, judge, saviour, servant. Over the centuries artists have represented him in every style and attitude for there is no one way of presenting the one Christ. Each person has an image that touches more deeply than another. The heart leaps at the sight and is inspired in a moment of recognition. The image outside corresponds to the image already hidden within. The inmost self, the true self, the Christ-nature, is revealed, and the meditator now knows consciously what was known obscurely. The Spirit has spoken to the spirit in the heart and the Christ is conceived in the depths of faith.

However, there may be no representation from the past or even a word in the gospels that rings completely true. Every person must discover the particular way in which the Spirit reveals the Christ to them. The meditator cannot rely just on what others have seen but must discover new vistas. The Christ must be discovered in new ways or the real self will remain obscure.

In the quiet of meditation no obstacle is placed to the work of the Spirit who inspires anew in every age and reveals aspects of Christ as varied as the variety of human experience. Out of the silence an aspect of Christ will appear, perhaps a visual image or a scene or an emotion or a word, which rouses the meditator.

If the aspect does not touch and lead to a deep satisfaction, the meditator needs to re-enter the quiet. If the aspect is not immediately recognized as of Christ, it should at least be compatible with what is known of Christ from the gospels. It is the resonance which counts.

When the rousing aspect does come to us, the meditator stays with it and contemplates and enjoys it, for it is the revelation of both Jesus and the self. At that moment the meditator knows themselves and Jesus. It is the one Self that is known.

A poem

I searched in the dense thickets and roamed the open
    plains, seeking a place to rest.
It was a long journey, with winding ways and a baulking at
    the cliff.
But suddenly you appeared, stepping out from behind the
    trees.
And I recognized you, my friend, companion at my side,
    citizen of my soul,
and knew myself — for are we not one being?

2. The face of suffering

Jesus then came out wearing the crown of thorns and the purple robe. Pilate said, 'Here is the man'. (John 19.5)

The shroud of Turin, whatever its puzzling origin, portrays better than any artist how Jesus would have seemed in death. The face possesses an interiority and a calm majesty, even as it shows the signs of beating: the swollen cheek, the trickle of blood. Marks of flagellation are seen on the chest. This image powerfully leads the viewer to the same interior calm, to the great strength that can endure such intense suffering. It teaches the attitude, which alone can take on the sins of the world. The shroud is a visual form of the Gospel.

By contemplating the suffering Face all human suffering comes to the fore. The inner strength of the Face and its serenity communicate compassion for others. Further, by seeing the truth of the Face, the truth of all who suffer becomes clear. The meditator experiences neither anxiety at suffering nor indifference, no wish to cause pain or despair at experiencing it. Then while sensing the pain an inner light begins to dawn in the meditator who in turn becomes like the Man in the shroud, united to people in their suffering and communicating to them a calm serenity, neither ignorant of pain nor useless under its blows.

A poem

Where are you, sleeper in the dark,
what inner landscape do you perceive,
as you lie there in silence?
What calm, what quiet persists under the blows,
which bring you to yourself
and take us with you into the Void?

3. The face of the future

In a short time you will no longer see me and then a short time
later you will see me again. (John 16.16)

A person is not accountable for the face with which they are born, so it
is said, but deserve the face they have at the age of forty. Choices and
attitudes form the expression: sly or open, strong or hesitant. The face
may be beautiful when young but the faces of the old radiate an inner
beauty that is even more attractive. But what will our future appearance
be at the resurrection of the dead?

That question is not unanswerable, for the seeds of the future are
planted in the present.

How might one imagine Jesus if he were to come now before us?
How would he look: strong, soft, divine, human, young, old, dynamic,
gentle, glorious, suffering, tall, short, large, small? He will be none of
these and all of these.

What might one expect or want him to be; what would give happiness and satisfaction? For the Christ imagined by the meditator is the
person the meditator will be. The character one would want him to have
is the personality one wishes to acquire and which will be given, since
God 'fills the starving with good things' (Psalm 107.9).

The activity of this meditation is to visualize creatively, no matter
how sketchily, the Christ who is coming, to imagine the expression, the
inner quality, and then to dwell in this imagined presence. By imagining
the person of Christ the practitioner touches their own future and touches
the person who, in a sense, they already are.

4. The face of the Unseen

He who sees me sees the Father. (John 14.9)

The clay pot is an important symbol in India. It encloses space and by peering into the pot the meditator glimpses something of the Void at the heart of the universe.

The heart of Jesus is somewhat similar, for it encloses the infinite spaciousness of the One who is open to all, infinitely welcoming, who places no obstacles, who is boundless and unconfined, in whose expansiveness the dove can spread its wings and fly in every direction without constraint.

The contemplation of Christ's heart leads necessarily to the contemplation of the One who is the Void, who is the Silence from whom the Word springs. Indeed if the contemplation of the Christ does not lead to the One who is not Christ, then the Christ has not been properly contemplated.

The contemplation of the heart of Jesus leads to an awareness of the One in whose heart Jesus rests, for Jesus is the mediator who leads beyond the confines of the world and beyond himself to the welcoming cave of God's heart.

The lance was thrust into the heart of Jesus and opened it, allowing blood and water to flow. From the infinite recesses within, blessings flow in an unfailing stream. By contemplating the heart and observing the void within, the meditator comes to the Open Heart. The meditator's heart rests in Jesus' heart, which itself rests in the Sublime Heart.

By contemplating for a while the space delimited by the pot the meditator is taken into the Void. All imagining, all thought, disappears and all ambition ceases. The tranquility of the unmoving space is calming and leads to transcendence. So by contemplating the open vase of Jesus' pierced heart the meditator gazes into the intoxicating abyss of the Ineffable Heart and rests there.